William C. (William Caryl) Cornwell

The Currency and the Banking law of the Dominion of Canada

With Reference to Currency Reform in the United States

William C. (William Caryl) Cornwell

The Currency and the Banking law of the Dominion of Canada
With Reference to Currency Reform in the United States

ISBN/EAN: 9783337117337

Printed in Europe, USA, Canada, Australia, Japan

Cover: Foto ©Suzi / pixelio.de

More available books at **www.hansebooks.com**

THE CURRENCY AND THE BANKING LAW OF THE DOMINION OF CANADA

CONSIDERED WITH REFERENCE TO CURRENCY REFORM IN THE UNITED STATES

BY

WILLIAM C. CORNWELL

G. P. PUTNAM'S SONS

NEW YORK
27 WEST TWENTY-THIRD STREET

LONDON
24 BEDFORD STREET, STRAND

The Knickerbocker Press

1895

NOTE.

THE substance of the matter included under the head of the "Canadian Banking System—Its Growth and Present Operation" in the following pages was embodied in an address delivered at the American Bankers' Convention, New Orleans, on November 12, 1891. The situation in the United States, then portrayed, still continues, except that the repeal of the purchase clause has since been accomplished. The forecast of danger, made at that time, was realized during 1893. The attention of the whole country is now centred upon the struggle for currency reform.

The Banking Act of Canada is given entire in the second part of the book. The clauses and sections of especial interest, in view of reforms proposed, are printed in heavy-faced type.

CONTENTS.

THE CANADIAN BANKING SYSTEM—ITS GROWTH AND PRESENT OPERATION.

THE CANADIAN BANKING SYSTEM—ITS GROWTH AND PRESENT OPERATION.

INTRODUCTION, WRITTEN IN 1891—CONDITIONS IN THE UNITED STATES BEFORE REPEAL OF THE SILVER-PURCHASE CLAUSE.

THIS country is practically at sea on the currency question. We are pounding along like a great ship on the ocean, with the engines at their utmost, politics at the wheel, ignorant of our bearings, and liable at any moment to collision and disaster; for, what with an unpliable, inelastic circulating medium, much of it base in value and ground out mechanically and without scientific control, at the rate of four and a half millions per month, no one can say what the outcome will be.

THE PANIC PREDICTED.

At such times wise men glance abroad and backward to get, if possible, some light upon the dark waters from the past and present experiences of other nations. I desire in this paper to call the attention of such men to the experiences of our sister nation, Canada, on the grounds that, while being nearest to us geographically and physically, her conditions are the most closely allied to our own of any community that we know of.

LOOKING FOR LIGHT.

Canada has, for many years, existed under a banking law which, with additions and improvements from time to time, has given her a circulating medium fully meeting all the requirements of every season, both as to elasticity and safety, and to-day, with the improvement brought about by the amended law going into effect last July, she has, I believe, for her needs, the most perfect currency system of any nation in the world, except, perhaps, that of Scotland, after whose system her's is closely modelled. In fact, the Canadian partakes, in its character, of the sterling qualities of the Scotch system, just as the Canadians themselves possess many of the admirable characteristics of that grand people from whom they are largely descended or made up.

CANADA'S ADEQUATE BANKING LAWS.

AMERICAN EXPERIENCE WITH BANK NOTES.

Before entering upon the subject proper, it may be well to refer to the period of bank-note issues in the United States previous to the inauguration of our national system, as the disasters of that time and the wild and exciting incidents attending the progress, explosions, and final suppression of the State-bank issues seem to have planted a prejudice in the minds of Americans against any kind of individual bank issues without discrimination, notwithstanding that in several of the States the business was conducted with the utmost honor and com-

A PREJUDICE.

plete success. I may say that the prejudice was planted even farther back in the history of America by the burnt-child experience with the old Continental notes which were a dead loss to the enormous amount at that time of $196,000,000.

This was along in the latter part of the last century. Just before the final collapse, a desperate effort was made to hold up the currency, but notwithstanding all that the Government, aided by the leading men of that period, could do, a dozen eggs sold for $5000 in Continental paper money, and a silk hat of the period, which would be worth about $7.00, cost $140,000 in Continental currency The word was burned into the language, and then, as now, utter worthlessness of a thing was conveyed by the expression, "it is not worth a continental."

CONTINENTAL CURRENCY.

To many of you, the older members of this association, the fiery destruction of the State Bank-note era, in the South and West, the Wild-Cat period, as it is called, is still vivid. Those were times when the contents of a man's pocket-book would slowly burn to ashes through the failure of a dozen banks of issue in an hour, or, when the farther one went from home, the greater became the discount on the notes he carried with him, parented, as they were, by banks of no reputation beyond the town line where they happened to be situated.

WILD-CAT.

Even in those uncertain days the humor of the American

gave rise to that venerable story of the man who had started on a journey, and after he had proceeded about three miles, heard that a bank near by had failed. He ran all the way home to see if he had any bills on that bank, and when he got there found that he had n't any bills on that bank, or on any other bank.

NO BILLS AT ALL.

This was the time of the "Red Dog" bills, as they were called. Banks would locate temporarily in a place and issue bills. Then, when they had exhausted the resources of that community, would move overnight to a distant town and there, instead of having new bills printed, would use the old ones, simply stamping the name of the new locality on the old bills in red ink. Hence the name Red Dog.

RED DOG.

No wonder that after experiences of this kind, a nation should come to regard the very principle of State issue with holy horror, and should embrace the opposite extreme of a national and over-secured currency as an unalloyed blessing, refusing to consider anything else even at this late period, when the private profit and important public benefits of the system, as far as circulation is concerned, have as completely disappeared as the life from the leaves of winter.

THE OTHER EXTREME.

GROWTH OF THE CANADIAN SYSTEM.

I propose now to sketch briefly the growth of the Canadian system, to show how it developed gradually out of experience, guided by wisdom, avoiding the dangerous fungus growths always ready to spring up in the hot earth of financial legislation, and has come to be a sturdy and fruitful tree.

GROWTH OF THE CANADIAN SYSTEM.

In the old Province of Canada, before the formation of the Dominion, banking was done in a cautious and tentative way, and the skeleton structure for the present system was erected.

For a long time previous to 1866, banks under royal charter issued their own notes, to the amount of their paid-up capital, but these were fully secured by a deposit of public or government securities. This, you will perceive, is what is called specially secured circulation, and is the principle of our National Bank-note issue. It is well to observe that this experiment was tried by Canada long ago and formed a step toward the better plan of general security.

SPECIALLY SECURED CIRCULATION.

In 1866 a national currency was inaugurated and an attempt made to provide for a surrender by the banks of their right to issue. Fortunately, this did not succeed. National currency was issued, $8,000,000 at first, running up to $20,000,000 in 1880, secured by a 25 % reserve, but the banks not only held on to their rights, but procured an extension of them.

NATIONAL CURRENCY DEMANDED.

They were allowed to issue notes to the amount of their unimpaired paid-up capital, *without deposit of securities.* The tax on circulation, which had been one per cent., was removed. Other wise provisions were made,

PROGRESS.

and, as they still exist, I shall speak of them later on. Stockholders were held doubly liable.

In the year 1880 it became necessary to act upon the question of the renewal, or not, of bank charters which expired in 1881. It was a year which, in Canadian politics, more nearly resembled an American situation than any which that country has perhaps ever experienced. The fanatical element was partially unleashed, and was baying at the moon in that wild and deep-toned howl that we are so familiar with in this country. Tariff reform had won a victory, and the excitement of the contest extended into an agitation for a national currency.

AN AMERICAN SITUATION.

The agitation grew, and developed finally into a furor for "rag money," and a stampede against bank privileges.

If this is not an American situation, it will be hard to find one. Nevertheless, the very exigencies of the contest brought to the front the very best in the opposition, and the bankers and leading financial minds of the Dominion wrested from the fiery struggle a still more perfect bank act, which renewed charters for ten years more.

The crowning achievement at this time was the formulation of that clause in the act which, for the first time, made bank notes a prior lien on the assets of the bank—a first charge before all others. This was the ringing stroke, which drove home, once for all, the question of security, and made it sure. Some minor changes were made at this time.

THE CROWNING ACHIEVEMENT.

This was the Bank Act of 1880. Ten years later charters were to expire and a new act would be necessary. You will see how, step by step, the system was being improved. There was no wild rush from one new scheme to another. Beginning on a sure foundation, with deliberation, determination, and aided by the best and most thoroughly trained ability, the structure was growing steadily and solidly. And now the year 1890 once more reopened the question. This time there was no such outburst of the fanatical spirit manifested by the opposition ten years before. Some dangerous measures, to be sure, were proposed by the Government, but upon full explanation by the bankers of what the outcome would be these were abandoned. I quote now from the able address of Mr. George Hague, General Manager of the Merchants Bank of Canada, at the annual meeting of that institution last year, soon after the passage of the act. He says, in speaking of the conference between the Government and the bankers:

STEP BY STEP.

"The representations of the banks were received with all possible consideration by the Government, and their recommendations were generally adopted.

COURTESIES BY THE GOVERNMENT.

"The Government, however, had views of their own upon several matters which they courteously communicated for consideration. Some of these were considered so objectionable that we felt constrained to oppose them, not only in your interest, but in the public interest. . . .

DANGEROUS PROPOSALS.

"The proposal to compel the holding of a fixed reserve of money in proportion to their liabilities was demurred to by a large majority. It was pointed out that to insist upon the banks keeping locked up in their safes at all times any fixed sum of money would interfere with the rights of creditors, to meet whose demands all the banker's cash is held. It was shown that such a measure had never been tried in practice except in the United States, and that there, when banks attempted to keep the law, violent fluctuations in the rate of interest ensued. And, further, that circumstances occurred nearly every year that compelled them to disregard the law altogether.

FIXED RESERVE UNWISE.

"The proposal was withdrawn. .. . .

"During the progress of the bill through the House a remarkable absence of political feeling was manifest. Members of both parties gave themselves to the work of considering how to make the act as nearly perfect as possible."

POLITICAL FEELING BURIED.

I refer fully to these matters to show how differently financial legislation is conducted in Canada. It does seem as though this idea of legislation was the proper one—that is, to call in for advisement, when a subject is under consideration, the very highest authorities on that subject—in other words, the men whose experience, day by day for years, and whose thorough training entitles them to speak for this or that industry or profession. How different, perhaps, in the United States would be the condition of our own currency, if during past years the leading financiers and economists of the nation had had a prevailing voice in the matter.

TRUE METHODS OF LAW MAKING.

CANADIAN BANK ACT OF TO-DAY.

I come now to the Canadian Bank Act as it stands. It is a comprehensive piece of legislation, containing over one hundred clauses. Under its provisions, the banking of Canada is going on to-day in an even, effective manner, and the full requirements of business in the way of currency are met. I shall mention only the leading features, some of which have already been referred to.

THE BANK ACT OF TO-DAY.

First of all, banks of issue, the joint stock banks, and these are the only ones of which we are treating (there are, of course, in Canada, private banks and savings banks), must obtain their charters from Parliament, and must have a subscribed capital of $500,000, with at least $250,000 paid up.

CAPITAL.

The shareholders in these banks are doubly liable. That is, they can be called upon, in case of failure and deficit, for an amount in addition, equal to what they have already invested in the shares fully paid up.

DOUBLE LIABILITY.

No dividend is allowed which will impair the capital of the bank, and no dividend higher than 8 per cent. per annum, until a surplus or rest has been built up of at least 30 per cent.

RESTRICTED DIVIDENDS.

Monthly statements giving full particulars are to be furnished to the Government, and these are published in the daily papers, and, I need not say, scrutinized with much intelligence and interest by shareholders, depositors, and Canadian business men generally.

STATEMENTS.

An annual statement is furnished, with full details of profit and loss, to the yearly meeting of shareholders, and at these meetings the general manager usually delivers an address, and there is a common interchange of views.

In the interest of the Government, and in order to keep the Dominion notes in use, 40 per cent. of the reserve held by the banks is required to be so held in Dominion notes; and any bank making a payment up to $100 must, if so requested, pay in Dominion notes. (*No torn or defaced notes of any kind, either Government or bank, are allowed to be paid out.*)

DOMINION NOTES.

There are wise restrictions as to loans on real estate, etc., and regulations as to boards of directors. A bank has prior lien on warehouse merchandise, and on stocks and bonds, etc., and is given other privileges. Employees are not forgotten, authority being given to establish guarantee and pension funds out of the bank's holdings, for faithful servants.

PENSION FUNDS.

Examinations are not conducted by the Government, but under the branch system each bank has its Inspector General, who is a man of marked ability and skill, a thorough banker by education, advanced from the lowest round, a man who ranks next to the General Manager, and fully competent to take the latter's place. With examinations conducted by such men, the Canadian bank shareholders and depositors may well feel assured. I fear our National and State bank examinations would suffer by comparison.

EXAMINATIONS.

And now we come to the important provisions regarding note issues.

The amount of notes to be issued must never exceed the amount of unimpaired paid-up capital. NOTE ISSUES.

They are a first lien upon the assets of the bank, taking precedence even of Government claims.

The double liability of stockholders is a last resort to the bank itself in case all the other assets are not sufficient to pay the note holders.

But a new and additional security for notes was introduced in 1890, known as "The Bank Circulation Redemption Fund." This fund is made up of a contribution of five per cent. by each bank on the amount of its own notes in circulation for the twelve months previous to July first of each year (adjusted annually). SECURITY.

The fund is deposited with the Government (which allows upon it to the banks three per cent. per annum interest), and is for the special purpose of redeeming the notes of any suspended bank.

In case of suspension, notes of the suspended bank begin at once to draw interest at six per cent. until redeemed by the receiver of the failed bank. If not redeemed in two months in this way, the notes, with interest, are paid out of the redemption fund, which is reimbursed by the failed bank as soon as possible. In case of depletion of the fund it is to be made up again by contributions yearly of one per cent. of its past year's circulation by each bank. This interest bearing quality after SUSPENDED NOTES DRAW INTEREST.

suspension, imparts an investment value to the notes of broken banks, as, being absolutely secure, they would be eagerly cashed by banks desiring to earn the six per cent. Such notes might bear a premium, but they could not possibly fall to a discount.

There is no tax upon circulation.

REDEMPTION AGENCIES.

Each bank is required to appoint agencies for the redemption of its notes in the principal cities of Canada, covering all territory from one end of the Dominion to the other. This does away with the old condition which forced notes of far-off banks to a discount, making the currency National—a brilliant quality of our own national bank notes, imparted, however, in a different manner.

I have thus briefly enumerated the main features of this admirable system of banking and note issues. In order to fully appreciate its workings it must be understood that the branch system is a very necessary part of its operations, and that the notes of all the banks are sent in and redeemed daily, like checks.

BRANCH BANKING.

The branch system of banking has received little attention in the United States. Its effective operation in Canada is worthy of attention. And the conditions are so similar to our own that the study becomes an important one.

The great advantages of the system are now universally recognized among the people.

"There was a time in Canada, about twenty years ago," says Mr. B. E. Walker, General Manager of the Canadian Bank of Commerce, "when some people thought that in every town a bank, no matter how small, provided it had no branches and had its owners resident in the neighborhood, was a greater help to the town than the branch of a large and powerful bank. In those days, perhaps, the great banks were too autocratic, and had not been taught by competition to respect fully the wants of each community. If this feeling ever existed to any extent, it has passed away. I do not know any country in the world so well supplied with banking facilities as Canada. The branch system not only enables every town of one thousand or twelve hundred people to have a joint stock bank, but to have a bank with a power behind it generally twenty to fifty times greater than a small bank would have."

ITS GROWTH.

It is true that here is an element of danger—the danger of more credit to a small community than it can stand, and consequent ruin. Rare wisdom and firmness, and especially thorough training in the profession, are required to counteract this danger.

DANGERS.

But so convinced of the superior value of the branch system are the Canadians, that there are only seven banks which have no branches. The other 38 control about 400 bank offices.

These great banks of Canada each, with from ten to fifty branches, gather up the money lying idle in one locality and transmit it automatically to another locality which has enterprise enough to use it. It must be admitted that this is what the banks in our own country

ADVANTAGES.

do not do. There is no systematic distribution of money here. The consequence is that rates of interest may be four to six per cent. in the extreme East, and twelve to twenty per cent. in the West. This is not so in Canada. From one end of their broad domain to the other, from Quebec, Montreal, Toronto, Halifax to far Manitoba, the extreme variation in rates is not over two per cent.

On this part of the subject Mr. Walker says:

"In Canada we see the deposits of the saving classes applied directly to the country's new enterprises in a manner nearly perfect. The Bank of Montreal borrows money from depositors at Halifax and many points in the Maritime Provinces, where the savings largely exceed the new enterprises, and it lends money in Vancouver or in the Northwest, where the new enterprises far exceed the people's savings. In what other country is such a splendid development of banking to be seen as that involved in transferring the idle money of the Atlantic towns and cities to the new centres of enterprise on the Pacific. My own bank in the same manner gathers deposits in the quiet, unenterprising parts of Ontario, and lends the money in the enterprising localities, the whole result being that thirty-eight business centres, in no case having an exact equilibrium of deposits and loans, are able to balance the excess or deficiency of capital, economizing every dollar, the depositor obtaining a large rate of interest, and the borrower obtaining money at a lower rate than borrowers in any of the colonies of Great Britain, and a lower rate than in the United States, except in the very great cities in the East.

DISTRIBUTION.

LOW RATES.

"In Canada capital marches automatically across the continent to find the borrower, and the extra interest obtained scarcely pays the loss of time it would take to send it so far, were the machinery not so perfect."

In this way the interests of one part of the community are interwoven with those of another far away. The bank fulfils its proper function of carefully conserving the credit of the whole country and distributing it to the most worthy in the most economical manner possible. The interests of the bank are not local, but wide-spread. Its character becomes essentially and truly National. The system resembles a great centralizing reservoir, condensing the moisture from the vast areas where it exists in redundant quantities and dispersing it gently like summer rain over the arid plains. This is the fulfilment of one of the great fundamental ideas of modern banking. What was begun to be done away back in the seventeenth century by the goldsmiths of London is perfected in the branch system of banking in Canada to-day.

NATIONAL CHARACTER IMPARTED.

We come now in our investigation of the workings of the Canadian bank-note system to the important relation between the branch system and the note issues. The Canadian banks have a right to issue bank notes, as we have seen, to the extent of their unimpaired paid-up capital; but this right would be of little value if these notes could not be gotten into general circulation. And if each bank had but its one head office, little headway could be made in this direction, as the notes are subject to daily redemption, and, in order to keep afloat as much as

BRANCHES AND THE NOTE ISSUE.

possible of its own issue, each bank sends in daily, for redemption, all the notes of other banks which come into it. But, under the branch system, the head office supplies its branches with all the till or teller's money they may need—money for the payment of local checks, pay-rolls, etc., etc.—by sending out to it notes of its own issue. The advantage of all this is that the till money, the cash reserve of the branches costs no interest, and is a source of large profit to the bank of issue. And here is the inducement for the formation of branches, and without which the growth of the branch system would be much stunted. You will see at once that all this is rendered possible by the fact that the bank-note issue is secured by the general assets of the bank, and costs no interest. Whereas, if specially secured, as are our own national bank notes, it would take actual capital to buy the securities, and at the present low rate of governments would be unprofitable.

TILL MONEY.

GENERAL VERSUS SPECIAL SECURITY.

This point is so important that I desire to make it very clear. A correspondent in Canada writes:

"In the United States it probably does not occur to the banker to make any distinction between the money in the teller's drawers or tills and the money kept in reserve in the safes, or, as we call them, treasuries. In this country there is the greatest possible difference. All of the cash used by a bank in the United States is really money to the bank—that is, it costs the loss of interest to carry it idle. So far as this idle cash is

A SAVING OF INTEREST.

necessary as a reserve the loss of interest should be borne, but to the extent that it is necessary only as machinery for paying cheques or other change-making purposes, it is, in our opinion, a wasteful and unscientific system. If you look at the figures of cash held by the Canadian banks, the amount appears wretchedly small in proportion to the liabilities. But, as a matter of fact, the cash there shown is only the gold and legal-tender reserves in the treasuries and the trifling amount of gold and legal tenders kept in the tills for the convenience of customers. The main business of making payments in money is done by the note issues of the bank. I notice that it takes from about $1,500,000 to $2,000,000 of our notes to keep the tills of all the branch offices filled with cash. This has the advantage of costing no interest, and, inasmuch as it does not represent a liability of the bank until actually issued, it does not show in our published statements. If it were a specially secured currency, we would at the moment appear as having issued about the $4,000,000 we are entitled to under law, and as holding $1,500,000 to $2,000,000 of this same money in cash in our tills."

USEFULNESS OF THE NOTE ISSUES AT THE BRANCHES.

SECURITY.

I desire now to dwell for a moment, and in conclusion, upon the two most important features of any currency, namely: the features of Security and of Elasticity; and to see how far and how perfectly they exist in the Canadian system. We have found that for security the Canadian bank note has, first, the entire amount of the assets of the bank; second, the double liability of the stockholder; and, third, the Bank Circulation Redemption

TWO IMPORTANT FEATURES.

Fund. This redemption fund will average something between a million and a half and two million dollars. It is sufficient to say that in no failure which Canada has ever had under the present system, would one dollar of this fund have been touched.

SECURITY.

In a letter to me on this subject, Mr. George Hague writes:

"The provision making notes a preferential claim against all assets came into force some years ago, and it has proved itself capable of standing the strongest strain that has been put upon it. The test of a measure like this is, of course, to be found when a bank which has been exceptionally badly managed stops payment. Now, we have had three instances of the kind during the last ten years. In each of these there had been the most scandalous mismanagement conceivable, with not a little of the element of fraud. Yet, in every instance, the notes had been redeemed in full. The only loss being the holding of them for a shorter or longer time. In two instances the notes were redeemed within one or two months. In the other instance, which was by far the worst of the three, a longer delay took place.

EXPERIENCES AND TESTS.

"In amending the Bank Act recently, the banks voluntarily proposed, in order to meet any possible objection, and to make assurance doubly sure, to provide a safety fund to be contributed to by all the banks and held by the Government, to apply to the redemption of notes. The greater part of the banking fraternity considered this entirely unnecessary. That is my own view. But we were willing to go as far as possible, to meet any possible objection to the continuance of our circulation on its present basis."

REDEMPTION FUND NOT NECESSARY.

And going back into the other security—the Assets; on the 30th of September of this year, when the latest returns of the Canadian Chartered Banks was published, the latter had assets with the double liability added of $334,384,438 to take care of $34,083,051 circulation, which means an average of $9.80 for every dollar of circulation, or taking the case of the lowest individual percentage, of assets to circulation, $5.00 back of every one dollar in notes.

A STARTLING FACT.

Let this be written in large letters: EVERY DOLLAR IN CANADIAN BANK NOTES HAS OVER NINE DOLLARS (on the average) IN SECURITY BACK OF IT TO MAKE IT GOOD.

And yet along the border, two or three years ago, an over-zealous revenue organization succeeded in twisting the ten per cent. penalty of the National Bank Act against these same Canadian notes, giving a meaning to the law which it has been conclusively proved it never was intended to have by the broad and intelligent framers of that act, practically banishing the Canadian bills from the useful position which they had occupied as furnishing a convenient and absolutely safe medium of exchange at the border between two friendly nations.

ELASTICITY.

I think we have thoroughly settled the question of SECURITY. But let a currency be ever so secure, if it does not meet the requirements of trade, if it has no elasticity, it is a comparatively dead factor. That, unfortunately, is the condition to-day of our own national bank currency. Its issue was a war measure, adopted for the purpose of placing Government loans, which were badly needed, and paid for at high interest. It did certainly once for all wipe out the wide-spread evil of the wild-cat issue ; but it was a war measure, born out of the smoke of battle, and birth-marked by the abnormal pressure of the times. It fought well, it did its duty grandly, but what wonder that when the smoke cleared away and the piping times of peace came again and we looked at it with calm, deliberate eye, it turned out to be a dwarfed and twisted creature, unfit for any work but that of war, and shrinking away into uselessness in the sunlight of the eternal fitness of things. The national bank currency was absolutely secure. It was profitable to the banks with Government bonds at a high rate of interest. But it had no elasticity. Its tendency, because of the great profit in it, and because the country was off the specie payment basis, and there was no pressure to redeem, was towards inflation, and a limit had to be put upon it. Then came the decrease in Government interest rates, and currency issue became unprofitable. Shrinkage followed. From the highest point of $360,000,000, towards which it ranged, it has shrunken down now in the last ten years to $120,000,000, and left a great gap which has, in turn, opened the way to a great danger.

NATIONAL CURRENCY A WAR MEASURE.

SHRINKAGE.

How has the great gap left by the shrinkage of the National Currency in the last ten years from $360,000,000 to $120,000,000 been filled? How has this great shrinkage been met when the currency requirements of trade have yearly been growing greater? Not by bringing to bear upon the question the greatest wisdom and skill of trained financiers, not with a deliberate consideration of how to promote the best interests of commerce on a scientific basis. It has been met by Politics and not by Science. It has been met with an eye to votes and the spoils and much indifference as to what might be the greatest good to the greatest number. It has been met by the Silver Miner, who has hoisted his pickaxe upon his shoulder and marched to Washington with a great and uproarious following of rag-money shouters and currency doctors and misguided western farmers, and many honest people besides, who, knowing that the country needed currency, and with half-formed ideas of bi-metallism, have with the others and altogether between them plunged the country in the last few years into a wretched slough of silver—a morass of three hundred and fifty millions of tokens worth seventy-five cents on the dollar; and they are still clamoring for free coinage, and after that they will want *free money*.

HOW MET.

THE POLITICIAN AND THE SILVER MINER.

A PALPABLE DIFFERENCE.

And so nobody claims that the National Bank currency possesses or ever did possess the feature of elasticity. It was an expedient, brilliant, but not intended to be scientific, hastening towards inflation at one time, excited by a relish for profit, and only controlled by an arbitrary act of Congress, and then, with the profit struck out of it, it shrank away steadily without any reference to trade requirements at all.

We have left a splendid organization under efficient control, ready for a NEW SYSTEM.

On the other hand, let us turn to our calm friends, the Canadians, and see how the test of elasticity is met by their note-issues. The scientific basis of elasticity is this: *There must be some inducement or force for issue which will operate when trade requires the bank notes, and ceasing to operate when the trade requirement ceases, will extinguish the notes.* In the Canadian system the inducing force is the profit on notes issued, and the extinguishing power is the desire of each bank to float its own issues. Here let me once more refer to Mr. Walker's argument for a concise statement of the conditions in his country. He says:

ELASTICITY.

"In Canada, bank notes are secured by a first lien upon the entire assets in the bank, including the double liability, the security being general and not special, not by the deposit of Government bonds, for instance. Therefore, it is clear that it will always pay Canadian banks to issue currency when trade demands it. Because bank notes in Canada are issued against the general estate of the bank, they are subject to daily, *actual* redemption; and no bank dares to issue notes without reference to its power to redeem, any more than a solvent merchant dares to give promissory notes without reference to his ability to pay.

EBB AND FLOW.

The presentation for actual redemption of every note not required for purposes of trade, is assured by the fact that every bank seeks, by the activity of its own business, to keep out its own notes and, therefore, sends back daily for redemption the notes of all other banks. This great feature in our system is generally overlooked, but it is because of this daily actual redemption that we have never had any serious inflation of our currency, if indeed there ever has been any inflation at all. Trade, of course, becomes inflated, and the currency will follow trade, but that is a very different thing from the existence in a country of a great volume of paper money not required by trade. . . . In Canada it is not enough that the volume of currency should rise and fall from year to year; it must also, for about eight months in each year, keep at a minimum (excluding the legal tenders) of about $30,000,000, and for about two months of the remaining four reach $36,000,000 or $37,000,000, a sudden advance of 20 per cent., followed after a few weeks by as sudden a decline."

DAILY REDEMPTION.

SUDDEN ADVANCE AND DECLINE TO BE MET.

And quoting again from Mr. Hague's letter on the subject of whether in Canada the currency is always sufficient to care for the Autumnal Drain, he writes:

"With regard to the matter of our Canadian circulation, experience has proven that the feature of elasticity is completely provided for and that our currency during past years has shown itself capable of expansion sufficient for the largest demands that could be made upon it. The capital of some of the banks is so large that they have never circulated to anything near the amount that they were authorized by law. The reserve of circulation power in the banks unitedly is, therefore, considerably in excess of any demand made upon it. For example:

The total capital of the banks is	$60,740,000
The highest circulation ever reached was	38,000,000
The highest expansion during any fall season was . . .	7,000,000

So you will see it has never been necessary to issue more than about 60 per cent. of the amount of bank notes authorized by law. Panics for fear of stringency are thus unknown. The Canadians never know what it is to go through an American money-squeeze in the autumn.

THE AUTUMN MONEY SQUEEZE.

So much for the feature of ELASTICITY.

I have endeavored to show how scientific, how completely filling all the requirements of the community in which it exists and flourishes, is the Canadian bank and note system, and now, naturally, you ask me whether I advocate the adoption of this system in the United States. I have simply to say in reply that I am not here to advocate any system. Every thinking banker who has paid any attention to the subject, knows that our present system of currency is inadequate, and our condition in this regard very unsatisfactory, uncomfortable, and I think I may say dangerous. I believe it to be a time for reconstruction, not by politicians, but by the most skilled economic wisdom which we can call to our aid. In such a time, a deliberate consideration of the better systems in operation should do some good. I think I have shown that such a system, and one of the best in the world, is in successful operation very near us, under conditions very nearly resembling our own,

CONCLUSION.

its arteries stretching over a vast country and carrying the life blood of commerce to hamlet and town and metropolis, building up worthy enterprises, and furthering and sustaining a healthy prosperity among the sturdy people of our sister nation, Canada.

THE BANKING ACT OF THE DOMINION OF CANADA, 1891.

THE BANKING ACT

OF

THE DOMINION OF CANADA.

1891.

53 VICTORIA.

CHAP. 31.

An Act respecting Banks and Banking.

[*Assented to 16th May, 1890.*]

HER Majesty, by and with the advice and consent of the Senate and House of Commons of Canada, enacts as follows:

SHORT TITLE.

SHORT TITLE. **1.** This Act may be cited as "*The Bank Act.*"

INTERPRETATION.

INTERPRETATION. **2.** In this Act, unless the context otherwise requires,—

"THE BANK." (*a.*) The expression "the bank" means any bank to which this Act applies;

"TREASURY BOARD." (*b.*) The expression "Treasury Board" means the board provided for by section nine of chapter twenty-eight of the Revised Statutes of Canada, or any Act in amendment thereof or substitution therefor;

(*c.*) The expression "goods, wares and merchandise" includes, in addition to the things usually understood thereby, timber, deals, boards, staves, saw-logs and other lumber, petroleum, crude oil, and all agricultural produce and other articles of commerce;

"GOODS, WARES AND MERCHANDISE."

(*d.*) The expression "warehouse receipt" means any receipt given by any person for any goods, wares, or merchandise, in his actual, visible and continued possession, as bailee thereof, in good faith, and not as of his own property, and includes receipts given by any person who is the owner or keeper of a harbor, cove, pond, wharf, yard, warehouse, shed, storehouse or other place for the storage of goods, wares or merchandise, for goods, wares and merchandise delivered to him as bailee and actually in the place, or in one or more of the places owned or kept by him, whether such person is engaged in other business or not;

"WAREHOUSE RECEIPT."

(*e.*) The expression "bill of lading" includes all receipts for goods, wares or merchandise, accompanied by an undertaking to transport the same from the place where they were received to some other place, whether by land or water, or partly by land and partly by water, and by any mode of carriage whatever;

"BILL OF LADING."

(*f.*) The word "manufacturer" includes maltsters, distillers, brewers, refiners and producers of petroleum, tanners, curers, packers, canners of meat, pork, fish, fruit or vegetables, and any person who produces by hand, art, process or mechanical means any goods, wares or merchandise.

MANUFACTURER.

APPLICATION OF ACT.

3. The provisions of this Act apply to the several banks enumerated in Schedule A to this Act, and to every bank incorporated after the first day of January, in the year one thousand eight hundred and ninety, whether this Act is specially mentioned in its Act of incorporation or not, but not to any other bank, except as hereinafter specially provided.

TO WHAT BANKS THE ACT APPLIES.

4. The charters or Acts of incorporation, and any Acts in amendment thereof, of the several banks enumerated in Schedule A to this Act are continued in force, so far as regards the incorporation and corporate name, the amount of capital stock, the amount of each share of such stock and the chief place of business of each bank, until the first day of July, in the year one thousand nine hundred and one, subject to the right of each bank to increase or reduce its capital stock in the manner hereinafter provided; and as to all other particulars this Act shall form and be the charter of each of the said banks until the said first day of July, in the year one thousand nine hundred and one,—subject in the case of La Banque du Peuple to the provisions hereinafter made in respect to that bank: Provided always, that the said charters or Acts of incorporation are hereby continued in force only in so far as they, or any of them, are not forfeited or rendered void under the terms thereof, or of this Act, or of any other Act passed or to be passed, by reason of the non-performance of the conditions thereof, or by insolvency, or otherwise.

CHARTERS CONTINUED TO 1ST JULY, 1901.

AS TO OTHER PARTICULARS.

PROVISO: AS TO FORFEITURE.

5. All the provisions of this Act, except those contained in sections three, six to seventeen (both inclusive), nineteen to twenty-seven (both inclusive), thirty-three, forty-five, and eighty-nine to ninety-six (both inclusive), apply to La Banque du Peuple: Provided, that wherever the word "directors" is used in any of the sections which apply to the said bank, it shall be read and construed as meaning the principal partners or members of the corporation of the said bank; and so much of the Act incorporating the said bank, or of any Act amending or continuing it, as is inconsistent with any section of this Act applying to the said bank, or which makes any provision in any matter provided for by such sections other than such as is hereby made, is hereby repealed; otherwise the said Acts are continued in force, subject to the proviso contained in section four of this Act.

WHAT PROVISIONS SHALL APPLY TO LA BANQUE DU PEUPLE.

PROVISO: AS TO DIRECTORS.

INCONSISTENT ENACTMENTS REPEALED.

6. The provisions contained in sections two, seven, thirty-seven, forty-seven to eighty-eight (both inclusive), and ninety-seven to one hundred and four (both inclusive), apply to the Bank of British North America and the Bank of British Columbia respectively; and the provisions contained in the other sections of this Act do not apply to the said banks.

WHAT PROVISIONS SHALL APPLY TO THE BANKS OF BRITISH NORTH AMERICA AND OF B.C.

7. For the purposes of the several sections of this Act made applicable to the Bank of British North America and the Bank of British Columbia, the chief office of the Bank of British North America shall be the office of the bank at Montreal, in the Province of Quebec, and the chief office of the Bank of British Columbia shall be the office of the bank at Victoria, in the Province of British Columbia.

CHIEF SEAT OF BUSINESS OF THE SAID BANKS.

8. The provisions of this Act may be extended to the Merchants' Bank of Prince Edward Island by the Treasury Board, upon the application of the directors of the said bank, before the expiration of the present charter of the said bank; and upon publication in the *Canada Gazette* of the resolution of the directors applying hereunder, and of the minute of the Treasury Board thereon allowing such application, the provisions of this Act shall, from the time named in such minute, or if there is no time named therein, from the date of the publication thereof in the *Canada Gazette*, apply to the said bank; and its charter and Act of incorporation, and any Acts in amendment thereof, shall thereupon be extended for the same time and to the extent as if the name of the said bank had been included in Schedule A to this Act.

HOW MERCHANTS' BANK OF P. E. I. MAY COME UNDER THIS ACT.

INCORPORATION AND ORGANIZATION OF BANKS.

9. The capital stock of every bank hereafter incorporated, the name of the bank, the place where its chief office is to be situate, and the name of the provisional directors shall be declared in the Act of incorporation of every such bank:

MATTERS TO BE PROVIDED FOR IN SPECIAL ACT.

FORM OF ACT OF INCORPORATION.

2. An Act of incorporation of a bank in the form set forth in Schedule B to this Act shall be construed to confer upon the bank thereby incorporated all the powers, privileges and immunities, and to subject it to all the liabilities and provisions set forth in this Act.

CAPITAL STOCK AND SHARES.

10. The capital stock of any bank hereafter incorporated shall be not less than five hundred thousand dollars, and shall be divided into shares of one hundred dollars each.

PROVISIONAL DIRECTORS.

11. The number of provisional directors shall be not less than five nor more than ten, and they shall hold office until directors are elected by the subscribers to the stock, as hereinafter provided.

OPENING OF STOCK BOOKS.

12. For the purpose of organizing the bank, the provisional directors may cause stock books to be opened, after giving public notice thereof,—upon which stock books shall be recorded the subscriptions of such persons as desire to become shareholders in the bank; and such books shall be opened at the place where the chief office of the bank is to be situate, and elsewhere, in the discretion of the provisional directors, and may be kept open for such time as they deem necessary.

FIRST MEETING OF SUBSCRIBERS.

NOTICE.

ELECTION OF DIRECTORS.

13. So soon as a sum not less than five hundred thousand dollars of the capital stock of the bank has been *bonâ fide* subscribed, and a sum not less than two hundred and fifty thousand dollars thereof has been paid to the Minister of Finance and Receiver General, the provisional directors may, by public notice, published for at least four weeks, call a meeting of the subscribers to the said stock, to be held in the place named in the Act of incorporation as the chief place of business of the bank, at such time and at such place therein as set forth in the said notice; at which meeting the subscribers shall determine the day upon which the annual general meeting of the bank is to be held, and shall elect such number of directors, duly qualified under this Act,

not less than five nor more than ten, as they think necessary, who shall hold office until the annual general meeting in the year next succeeding their election; and upon the election of directors as aforesaid the functions of the provisional directors shall cease.

14. The bank shall not issue notes nor commence the business of banking until it has obtained from the Treasury Board a certificate permitting it to do so, and no application for such certificate shall be made until directors have been elected by the subscribers to the stock in the manner hereinbefore provided; and every director, provisional director, or other person, issuing or authorizing the issue of the notes of such bank or transacting or authorizing the transaction of any business in connection with such bank, except such as is hereinbefore provided, before the obtaining of the certificate from the Treasury Board, shall be guilty of an offence against this Act.

CONDITIONS PREVIOUS TO COMMENCING BUSINESS BY NEW BANKS.

15. No certificate shall be given by the Treasury Board until it has shown to the satisfaction of the Board, by affidavit or otherwise, that all the requirements of this Act and of the special Act of incorporation of the bank, as to the payment required to be made to the Minister of Finance and Receiver General, the election of directors, deposit for security for note issue, or otherwise, have been complied with, and that the sum so paid was then held by the Minister of Finance and Receiver General; and no certificate as aforesaid shall be given except within one year from the passing of the Act of incorporation of the bank applying for the said certificate.

WHEN CERTIFICATE MAY BE GRANTED.

16. In the event of the bank not obtaining a certificate from the Treasury Board within one year from the time of the passing of its Act of incorporation, all the rights, powers and privileges conferred on such bank by its Act of incorporation shall thereupon cease and determine and be of no force and effect whatever.

IF CERTIFICATE IS NOT GRANTED.

17. Upon the issue of the certificate in manner hereinbefore provided, the Minister of Finance and Receiver General shall forth-

DISPOSAL OF AMOUNT DEPOSITED WITH MINISTER OF FINANCE.

with pay to the bank the amount of money so deposited with him as aforesaid, without interest, after deducting therefrom the amount required to be deposited under section fifty-four of this Act; and in case no certificate is issued by the Treasury Board within the time limited for the issue thereof, the amount so deposited shall be returned to the person depositing the same; but in no case shall the Minister of Finance and Receiver General be under any obligation to see to the proper application of the same in anyway.

INTERNAL REGULATIONS.

BY-LAWS MAY BE MADE.

18. The shareholders of the bank (or, in the case of La Banque du Peuple, the principal partners or members of the corporation thereof,) may regulate, by by-law, the following matters incident to the management and administration of the affairs of the bank, that is to say: The day upon which the annual general meeting of the shareholders for the election of directors shall be held; the record to be kept of proxies, and the time, not exceeding thirty days, within which proxies must be produced and recorded prior to a meeting in order to entitle the holder to vote thereon; the number of the directors, which shall not be less than five and not more than ten, and the quorum thereof, which shall not be less than three; their qualification, subject to the provisions hereinafter made; the method of filling vacancies in the board of directors whenever the same occur during each year, and the time and proceedings for the election of directors, in case of a failure of any election on the day appointed for it; the remuneration of the president, vice-president and other directors; and the amount of discounts or loans which may be made to directors, either jointly or severally, or to any one firm or person, or to any shareholder, or to corporations:

GUARANTEE AND PENSION FUNDS.

2. **The shareholders may authorize the directors to establish guarantee and pension funds for the officers and employees of the bank and their families, and to contribute thereto out of the funds of the bank:**

3. Until it is otherwise prescribed by by-law under this section, the by-laws of the bank on any matter which may be regulated by by-laws under this section shall remain in force, except as to any provision fixing the qualification of directors at an amount less than that prescribed by this Act; and no person shall be elected or continue to be a director unless he holds stock paid up to the amount required by this Act, or such greater amount as is required by any by-law in that behalf: CERTAIN BY-LAWS CONTINUED.

4. The foregoing provisions of this section, touching directors, shall not apply to La Banque du Peuple, which shall in these matters be governed by the provisions of its charter. BANQUE DU PEUPLE EXCEPTED.

19. The stock, property, affairs and concerns of the bank shall be managed by a board of directors, who shall be elected annually in manner hereinafter provided, and shall be eligible for re-election: BOARD OF DIRECTORS.

2. Each director shall hold capital stock of the bank as follows: —When the paid-up capital stock is one million dollars or less, each director shall hold stock on which not less than three thousand dollars has been paid up; when the paid-up capital stock is over one million dollars and does not exceed three million dollars, each director shall hold stock on which not less than four thousand dollars has been paid up; and when the paid-up capital stock exceeds three million dollars, each director shall hold stock on which not less than five thousand dollars has been paid up: QUALIFICATION.

3. A majority of the directors shall be natural-born or naturalized subjects of Her Majesty. MAJORITY TO BE BRITISH SUBJECTS.

4. The directors shall be elected by the shareholders on such day in each year as is appointed by the charter or by any by-law of the bank, and such election shall take place at the head office of the bank at such time of the day as the directors appoint; and public notice thereof shall be given by the directors, by publishing the same for at least four weeks previous to the time of holding such election, in a newspaper published at the place where the said head office is situate: ELECTION. NOTICE.

WHO SHALL BE DIRECTORS.

5. The persons, to the number authorized to be elected, who have the greatest number of votes at any election, shall be directors:

PROVISION IN CASE OF EQUALITY OF VOTES.

6. If it happens at any election that two or more persons have an equal number of votes and the election or non-election of one or more of such persons as a director or directors depends on such equality, then the directors who have a greater number, or the majority of them, shall determine which of the said persons so having an equal number of votes shall be the director or directors, so as to complete the full number; and the said directors, as soon as may be, after the said election, shall proceed to elect, by ballot, two of their number to be president and vice-president respectively:

ELECTION OF PRESIDENT, ETC.

VACANCIES, HOW FILLED.

7. If a vacancy occurs in the board of directors, such vacancy shall be filled in the manner provided by the by-laws; but the non-filling of the vacancy shall not vitiate the acts of a quorum of the remaining directors; and if the vacancy so created is in the office of the president or vice-president, the directors shall, from among themselves, elect a president or vice-president, who shall continue in office for the remainder of the year.

PROVISION IN CASE OF FAILURE OF ELECTION.

20. If an election of directors is not made on the day appointed for that purpose, such election of directors may take place on any other day, according to the by-laws made by the shareholders in that behalf; and the directors then in office shall remain in office until a new election is made.

MEETINGS OF DIRECTORS.

CASTING VOTE OF PRESIDING DIRECTOR.

21. At all meetings of the directors, the president, or in his absence the vice-president, or in the absence of both of them, one of the directors present, chosen to act *pro tempore*, shall preside; and the president, vice-president, or president *pro tempore* so presiding shall vote as a director, and if there is an equal division on any question shall also have a casting vote.

22. The directors may make by-laws and regulations (not repugnant to the provisions of this Act or the laws of Canada) touching the management and disposition of the stock, property, affairs and concerns of the bank, and touching the duties and conduct of the officers, clerks and servants employed therein, and all such other matters as appertain to the business of a bank: Provided always, that all by-laws of the bank heretofore lawfully made and now in force, in regard to any matter respecting which the directors may make by-laws under this section (including any by-laws for establishing guarantee and pension funds for the employees of the bank), shall remain in force until they are repealed or altered by others made under this Act.

GENERAL POWER OF DIRECTORS.

PROVISO: AS TO BY-LAWS IN FORCE.

23. The directors may appoint as many officers, clerks and servants for carrying on the business of the bank, and with such salaries and allowances, as they consider necessary, and they may also appoint a director or directors for any branch of the bank:

APPOINTMENT OF OFFICERS, ETC.

2. Before permitting any cashier, officer, clerk or servant of the bank to enter upon the duties of his office, the directors shall require him to give bond, guarantee, or other security to the satisfaction of the directors, for the due and faithful performance of his duties.

SECURITY TO BE GIVEN.

24. The directors of the bank, or any four of them,—or any number not less than twenty-five of the shareholders of the bank, who are together proprietors of at least one tenth of the paid-up capital stock of the bank, by themselves or by their proxies,—may, at any time, call a special general meeting of the shareholders, to be held at their usual place of meeting, upon giving six weeks' previous public notice, specifying in such notice the object of such meeting:

SPECIAL GENERAL MEETINGS.

2. If the object of any such special general meeting is to consider the proposed removal of the president or vice-president, or of a director of the bank, for maladministration or other specified and apparently just cause, and if a majority of the votes of the shareholders at such meeting is

REMOVAL OF PRESIDENT, DIRECTOR, ETC.

given for such removal, a director to replace him shall be elected or appointed in the manner provided by the by-laws of the bank, or if there are no by-laws providing therefor, then by the shareholders at such meeting; and if it is the president or vice-president who is removed, his office shall be filled by the directors in the manner provided in case of a vacancy occurring in the office of president or vice-president.

NEW ELECTION.

25. Every shareholder shall, on all occasions on which the votes of the shareholders are taken, have one vote for each share held by him for at least thirty days before the time of meeting; and in all cases when the votes of the shareholders are taken, the voting shall be by ballot:

VOTES ON SHARES.

BALLOT.

2. All questions proposed for the consideration of the shareholders shall be determined by the majority of the votes of the shareholders present in person or represented by proxy; and the chairman elected to preside at any such meeting of the shareholders shall vote as a shareholder only, unless there is a tie,—in which case, except as to the election of a director, he shall have a casting vote:

MAJORITY TO DETERMINE.

CASTING VOTE.

3. If two or more persons are joint holders of shares, any one of such joint holders may be empowered, by letter of attorney from the other joint holder or holders, or a majority of them, to represent the said shares, and vote accordingly:

AS TO JOINT HOLDERS OF SHARES.

4. Shareholders may vote by proxy, but no person other than a shareholder eligible to vote shall be permitted to vote or act as such proxy, and no manager, cashier, clerk, or other subordinate officer of the bank shall vote either in person or by proxy, or hold a proxy for that purpose:

PROXIES.

5. No appointment of a proxy to vote at any meeting of the shareholders of the bank shall be valid for that purpose unless it has been made or renewed in writing within the two years next preceding the time of such meeting:

RENEWAL OF PROXIES.

6. No shareholder shall vote, either in person or by proxy, on any question proposed for the consideration of the shareholders of the bank at any meeting of such shareholders, or in any case in which the votes of the shareholders of the bank are taken, unless he has paid all calls made by the directors which are then due and payable.

IN CERTAIN CASES CALLS MUST BE PAID BEFORE VOTING.

CAPITAL STOCK.

26. The capital stock of the bank may be increased from time to time, by such percentage or by such amount, as is determined upon by by-law passed by the shareholders, at the annual general meeting, or at any special general meeting called for the purpose: Provided always, that no such by-law shall come into operation, or be of any force or effect, unless and until a certificate approving thereof has been issued by the Treasury Board.

INCREASE OF CAPITAL.

APPROVAL OF TREASURY BOARD.

2. No such certificate shall be issued by the Treasury Board unless application therefor is made within three months from the time of the passing of such by-law, nor unless it appears to the satisfaction of the Treasury Board that a copy of such by-law, together with notice of intention to apply for such certificate, has been published for at least four weeks in the *Canada Gazette*, and in one or more newspapers published in the place where the chief office or place of business of the bank is situate; nothing herein contained, however, shall be construed to prevent the Treasury Board from refusing to issue such certificate if it thinks best so to do.

CONDITIONS OF APPLICATION FOR APPROVAL.

27. Any of the original unsubscribed capital stock, or of the increased stock of the bank, shall, when the directors so determine, be allotted to the then shareholders of the bank *pro ratâ*, and at such rate as is fixed by the directors, but no fraction of a share shall be so allotted; provided that in no case shall a rate be fixed by the directors, which will make the premium (if any) paid or payable on such stock so allotted exceed the percentage which the reserve fund of the bank then bears to the

HOW STOCK SHALL BE ALLOTTED.

paid-up capital stock thereof; and any of such allotted stock which is not taken up by the shareholder to whom such allotment has been made, within six months from the time when notice of the allotment was mailed to his address, or which he declines to accept, may be offered for subscription to the public, in such manner and on such terms as the directors prescribe.

CAPITAL STOCK MAY BE REDUCED.

28. The capital stock of the bank may be reduced by by-law passed by the shareholders at the annual general meeting, or at a special general meeting called for the purpose; but no such by-law shall come into operation or be of force or effect until a certificate approving thereof has been issued by the Treasury Board:

CERTIFICATE OF TREASURY BOARD.

2. No such certificate shall be issued by the Treasury Board unless application therefor is made within three months from the time of the passing of the by-law, nor unless it appears to the satisfaction of the Board that the shareholders voting for such by-law represent a majority in value of all the shares then issued by the bank, and that a copy of the by-law, together with notice of intention to apply to the Treasury Board for the issue of a certificate approving thereof, has been published for at least four weeks in the *Canada Gazette*, and in one or more newspapers published in the place where the chief office or place of business of the bank is situate; nothing herein contained, however, shall be construed to prevent the Treasury Board from refusing to issue such certificate if it thinks best so to do:

STATEMENTS TO BE SUBMITTED.

3. In addition to evidence of the passing of the by-law and the publication thereof in the manner above provided, statements showing the amount of stock issued and the number of shareholders, with the amount of stock held by each, represented at such meeting, and the number of shareholders, with the amount of stock held by each, who voted for such by-law, and also full statements of the assets and liabilities of the bank, together with a statement of the reasons and causes why such reduction is sought, shall be laid before the Treasury Board at the time of the application for the issue of a certificate approving such by-law.

4. The passing of such by-law, and any reduction of the capital stock of the bank thereunder, shall not, in any way, diminish or interfere with the liability of the shareholders of the bank to the creditors thereof at the time of the issue of the certificate approving such by-law: REDUCTION NOT TO AFFECT LIABILITY OF SHAREHOLDERS.

5. If, in any case, legislation is sought to sanction any reduction of the capital stock of any bank, a copy of the by-law or resolution passed by the shareholders in regard thereto, together with statements similar to those above provided to be laid before the Treasury Board, shall be filed with the Minister of Finance and Receiver General, at least one month prior to the introduction into Parliament of the Bill relating to such reduction: IF LEGISLATION IS ASKED TO SANCTION REDUCTION.

6. **The capital shall not be reduced below the amount of two hundred and fifty thousand dollars of paid-up stock.** LIMIT TO REDUCTION.

SHARES AND CALLS.

29. The shares of the capital stock of the bank shall be personal estate, and shall be assignable and transferable at the chief place of business of the bank, or at such of its branches, or at such place or places in the United Kingdom, or in any of the British colonies or possessions, and according to such form, and subject to such rules and regulations, as the directors prescribe; and books of subscription may be opened, and the dividends accruing on any shares of such stock may be made payable at any of the places aforesaid; and the directors may appoint such agents in the United Kingdom, or in any of the British colonies or possessions, for the purposes of this section, as they deem necessary. SHARES AND TRANSFER THEREOF. BOOKS OF SUBSCRIPTION.

30. The shares of the capital stock shall be paid in by such instalments and at such times and places as the directors appoint: Provided always, that the directors may cancel any subscription for any share unless a sum equal to ten per cent. at least on the amount subscribed for is actually paid at the time of, or within thirty days after, the time of subscribing; but such cancellation shall not PAYMENT OF SHARES. PROVISO: TEN PER CENT. PAYABLE ON SUBSCRIPTION.

relieve the subscriber from his liability to creditors in the event of insolvency as hereinafter provided.

31. The directors may make such calls of money from the several shareholders for the time being, upon the shares subscribed for by them respectively, as they find necessary:

CALLS ON SHARES.

2. Such calls shall be made at intervals of not less than thirty days, and upon notice to be given at least thirty days prior to the day on which such call shall be payable; and no such call shall exceed ten per cent. of each share subscribed.

TIME OF CALLS AND NOTICE.

LIMITATION.

32. The directors may, in case of the non-payment of any call, in the corporate name of the bank, sue for, recover, collect and get in all such calls, or may cause and declare such shares to be forfeited to the bank.

RECOVERY OF CALLS.

33. If any shareholder refuses or neglects to pay any instalment upon his shares of the capital stock at the time appointed therefor, such shareholder shall incur a penalty to the use of the bank of a sum of money equal to ten per cent. on the amount of such shares; and if the directors declare any shares to be forfeited to the bank they shall, within six months thereafter, without any previous formality other than thirty days' public notice of their intention so to do, sell at public auction the said shares, or so many of the said shares as shall, after deducting the reasonable expenses of the sale, yield a sum of money sufficient to pay the unpaid instalments due on the remainder of the said shares and the amount of penalties incurred upon the whole; and the president or vice-president, manager or cashier of the bank shall execute the transfer to the purchaser of the shares so sold; and such transfer shall be as valid and effectual in law as if it had been executed by the original holder of the shares thereby transferred; but the directors, or the shareholders at a general meeting, may, notwithstanding anything in this section contained,

FORFEITURE OF SHARES FOR NON-PAYMENT OF CALLS.

SALE IN SUCH CASE.

AND TRANSFER.

PROVISO.

remit, either in whole or in part, and conditionally or unconditionally, any forfeiture or penalty incurred by the non-payment of instalments as aforesaid, or the bank may enforce the payment of any call or calls by suit, instead of declaring the shares forfeited.

34. In any action brought to recover any money due on any such call it shall not be necessary to set forth the special matter in the declaration or statement of claim, but it shall be sufficient to allege that the defendant is holder of one share or more, as the case may be, in the capital stock of the bank, and is indebted to the bank for a call or calls upon such share or shares, in the sum to which the call or calls amount, as the case may be, stating the amount and number of such calls, whereby an action has accrued to the bank to recover the same from such defendant by virtue of this Act; and it shall not be necessary to prove the appointment of the directors.

RECOVERY BY SUIT.

WHAT ONLY NEED BE PROVED.

TRANSFER AND TRANSMISSION OF SHARES.

35. No assignment or transfer of the shares of the capital stock of the bank shall be valid unless it is made and registered and accepted by the person to whom the transfer is made, in a book or books kept for that purpose, nor unless the person making the same has, if required by the bank, previously discharged all his debts or liabilities to the bank which exceed in amount the remaining stock, if any, belonging to such person, valued at the then current rate; and no fractional part of a share, or less than a whole share, shall be assignable or transferable.

CONDITIONS OF TRANSFER OF SHARES.

FRACTION OF SHARE NOT TRANSFERABLE.

36. A list of all transfers of shares registered each day in the books of the bank, showing the parties to such transfers and the number of shares transferred in each case, shall be made up at the end of each day and kept at the chief place of business of the bank, for the inspection of its shareholders.

LIST OF TRANSFERS TO BE KEPT.

37. All sales or transfers of shares, and all contracts and agreements in respect thereof, hereafter made or purporting to be made,

TRANSFERRER OF SHARES MUST BE REGISTERED OWNER.

shall be null and void (saving however, as to a purchaser not having knowledge of the defect, his rights and remedies under the contract of sale), unless the person making such sale or transfer, or in whose name or on whose behalf the same is made, is at the time thereof the registered owner in the books of the bank of the share or shares so sold or transferred, or intended or purported so to be, or has the registered owner's assent to the sale, and the distinguishing number or numbers of such share or shares, if any, shall be designated in the contract or agreement of sale or transfer; and any person, whether principal, broker or agent, who violates the provisions of this section by wilfully selling or transferring, or attempting to sell or transfer, any share or shares by a false number, or of which the principal is not, at the time of such sale or attempted sale, the registered owner, or acting with the registered owner's assent to the sale, shall be guilty of an offence against this Act.

SALE OF SHARES UNDER EXECUTION.

38. When any share of the capital stock has been sold under a writ of execution, the officer by whom the writ was executed shall, within thirty days after the sale, leave with the bank an attested copy of the writ, with the certificate of such officer indorsed thereon, certifying to whom the sale has been made; and thereupon (but not until after all debts and liabilities of the holder of the share to the bank, and all liens existing in favor of the bank thereon, have been discharged, as herein provided), the president, vice-president, manager or cashier of the bank shall execute the transfer of the share so sold to the purchaser; and such transfer shall be, to all intents and purposes, as valid and effectual in law as if it had been executed by the holder of the said share.

TRANSMISSION OF SHARES OTHERWISE THAN BY TRANSFER, HOW AUTHENTICATED.

39. If the interest in any share in the capital stock becomes transmitted in consequence of the death, bankruptcy, or insolvency of any shareholder, or in consequence of the marriage of a female shareholder, or by any other lawful means than by a transfer according to the provisions of this Act, such transmission shall be authenticated by a declaration in writing, as hereinafter mentioned, or in

such other manner as the directors of the bank require; and every such declaration shall distinctly state the manner in which and the person to whom such shares have been transmitted, and shall be made and signed by such person; and the person making and signing such declaration shall acknowledge the same before a judge of a court of record, or before the mayor, provost or chief magistrate of a city, town, borough or other place, or before a notary public, where the same is made and signed; and every declaration so signed and acknowledged shall be left with the cashier, manager or other officer or agent of the bank, who shall thereupon enter the name of the person entitled under such transmission in the register of shareholders; and until such transmission has been so authenticated, no person claiming by virtue of any such transmission shall be entitled to participate in the profits of the bank, or to vote in respect of any such share of the capital stock: Provided always, that every such declaration and instrument as, by this and the next following section of this Act, are required to perfect the transmission of a share in the bank which is made in any country other than Canada, or any other British colony, or the United Kingdom, shall be further authenticated by the clerk of a court of record and under the seal of such court, or by the British consul or vice-consul, or other accredited representative of the British Government in the country where the declaration is made, or shall be made directly before such British consul or vice-consul or other accredited representative; and provided also, that the directors, cashier or other officer or agent of the bank may require corroborative evidence of any fact alleged in any such declaration.

PROVISO: AS TO DECLARATION MADE OUT OF CANADA, ETC.

PROVISO: FURTHER EVIDENCE MAY BE REQUIRED.

40. If the transmission of any share of the capital stock has taken place by virtue of the marriage of a female shareholder, the declaration shall be accompanied by a copy of the register of such marriage, or other particulars of the celebration thereof, and shall declare the identity of the wife with the holder of such share, and shall be made and signed by such female shareholder and her husband; and they

TRANSMISSION BY MARRIAGE OF FEMALE SHAREHOLDER.

may include therein a declaration to the effect that the share transmitted is the separate property and under the sole control of the wife, and that she may receive and grant receipts for the dividends and profits accruing in respect thereof, and dispose of and transfer the share itself, without requiring the consent or authority of her husband; and such declaration shall be binding upon the bank and persons making the same, until the said persons see fit to revoke it by a written notice to that effect to the bank; but the omission of a statement in any such declaration that the wife making the same is duly authorized by her husband to make the same shall not invalidate the declaration.

TRANSMISSION BY DECEASE.

41. If the transmission has taken place by virtue of any testamentary instrument, or by intestacy, the probate of the will, or the letters of administration, or act of curatorship or tutorship, or an official extract therefrom, shall, together with such declaration, be produced and left with the cashier or other officer or agent of the bank, who shall, thereupon, enter in the register of shareholders the name of the person entitled under such transmission.

FURTHER PROVISION IN SUCH CASE.

42. If the transmission of any share of the capital stock has taken place by virtue of the decease of any shareholder, the production to the directors and the deposit with them of an authentic notarial copy of the will of the deceased shareholder, if such will is in notarial form according to the law of the Province of Quebec, or of any authenticated copy of the probate of the will of the deceased shareholder, or of letters of administration of his estate, or of letters of verification of heirship, or of the act of curatorship or tutorship, granted by any court in Canada having power to grant the same, or by any court or authority in England, Wales, Ireland, or any British colony, or of any testament testamentary or testament dative expede in Scotland, or, if the deceased shareholder died out of Her Majesty's dominions, the production to and deposit with the directors of any authenticated copy of the probate of his will or letters of administration of his property, or other document of like import, granted by any court or authority having the requisite power in such matters, shall be sufficient justification and authority to the directors for paying any dividend, or for transferring or authorizing the transfer of any share, in pursuance of and in conformity to such probate, letters of administration, or other such document as aforesaid.

BANK NOT BOUND TO SEE TO TRUSTS.

43. The bank shall not be bound to see to the execution of any trust, whether express, implied or constructive, to which any share of its stock is subject; and the receipt of the person in whose name any such share stands in the books of the bank, or, if it stands in the name of more persons than one, the receipt of one of such persons shall be a sufficient discharge to the bank for any dividend or any other sum of money payable in respect of such share, unless express notice to the contrary has been given to the bank; and the bank shall not be bound to see to the application of the money paid upon such receipt, whether given by one of such persons or all of them.

EXECUTORS AND TRUSTEES NOT PERSONALLY LIABLE.

44. No person holding stock in the bank as executor, administrator, guardian or trustee, of or for any person named in the books of the bank as being so represented by him, shall be personally subject to any liability as a shareholder, but the estate and funds in his hands shall be liable in like manner and to the same extent as the testator, intestate, ward or person interested in such trust fund would be, if living and competent to hold the stock in his own name; and if the trust is for a living person, such person shall also himself be liable as a shareholder; but if such testator, intestate, ward or person so represented is not so named in the books of the bank, the executor, administrator, guardian or trustee shall be personally liable in respect of such stock as if he held it in his own name as owner thereof.

EXCEPTION.

ANNUAL STATEMENT AND INSPECTION.

STATEMENT TO BE LAID BEFORE ANNUAL MEETING.

45. At every annual meeting of the shareholders for the election of directors, the out-going directors shall submit a clear and full statement of the affairs of the bank, containing on the one part,—

The amount of the capital stock paid in, the amount of notes of the bank in circulation, the net profits made, the balances due to other banks, and the cash deposited in the bank, distinguishing deposits bearing interest from those not bearing interest; and on the other part,—

LIABILITIES.

The amount of the current coin, the gold and silver bullion, and the Dominion notes held by the bank, the balances due to the bank from other banks, the value of the real and other property of the bank, and the amount of debts owing to the bank, including and particularizing the amounts so owing upon bills of exchange, discounted notes, mortgages and other securities,—

ASSETS.

Exhibiting, on the one hand, the liabilities of, or the debts due by the bank, and on the other hand the assets and resources thereof; and the said statement shall also exhibit the rate and amount of the last dividend declared by the directors, the amount of reserved profits at the date of such statement, and the amount of debts due to the bank, over-due and not paid, with an estimate of the loss which will probably accrue thereon.

WHAT STATEMENT SHALL SHOW.

46. The books, correspondence and funds of the bank shall, at all times, be subject to the inspection of the directors; but no person, who is not a director, shall be allowed to inspect the account of any person dealing with the bank.

INSPECTION OF BOOKS, ETC.

DIVIDENDS.

47. The directors of the bank shall, subject to the provisions of this Act, declare quarterly or half yearly dividends of so much of the profits of the bank as to the majority of them seems advisable; and they shall give at least thirty days' public notice of the payment of such dividends previously to the date fixed for such payment; and they may close the transfer books during a certain time, not exceeding fifteen days, before the payment of each dividend.

DIVIDENDS.

48. No dividend or bonus shall ever be declared so as to impair the paid-up capital; and if any dividend or bonus is so declared or made payable, the directors who knowingly and wilfully concur therein shall be jointly and severally liable for the amount thereof as a debt due by them to the bank; and if any part of the paid-up capital is lost, the directors shall, if all the subscribed stock is not paid up, forthwith make calls upon the shareholders to an amount equivalent to such loss; and such loss and the calls, if any, shall be mentioned in the next return made by the bank to the Minister of Finance and Receiver General: Provided that, in any case in which the capital has been impaired as aforesaid, all net profits shall be applied to make good such loss.

DIVIDEND NOT TO IMPAIR CAPITAL.

CAPITAL LOST TO BE MADE UP.

PROVISO.

49. No division of profits, either by way of dividends or bonus, or both combined, or in any other way, exceeding the rate of eight per cent. per annum, shall be made by the bank, unless, after making the same, it has a rest or reserve fund equal to at least thirty per cent. of its paid-up capital; and all bad and doubtful debts shall be deducted before the amount of such rest is calculated.

DIVIDEND LIMITED UNLESS THERE IS A CERTAIN RESERVE.

RESERVES.

50. The bank shall hold not less than forty per cent. of its cash reserves in Dominion notes; and every bank holding at any time a less amount of its cash reserves in Dominion notes than is prescribed by this section shall incur a penalty of five hundred dollars for each and every violation of the provisions of this section:

PART OF RESERVE TO BE IN DOMINION NOTES.

PENALTY FOR NON-COMPLIANCE.

2. The Minister of Finance and Receiver General shall make such arrangements as are necessary for insuring the delivery of Dominion notes to any bank, in exchange for an equivalent amount of specie, at the several offices at which Dominion notes are redeemable, in the cities of Toronto, Montreal, Halifax, St. John, N. B., Winni-

SUPPLY OF DOMINION NOTES.

peg, Charlottetown and Victoria, respectively; and such notes shall be redeemable at the office for redemption of Dominion notes in the place where such specie is given in exchange.

NOTE ISSUE.

AMOUNT AND DENOMINATION OF BANK NOTES.

51. The bank may issue and re-issue notes payable to bearer on demand and intended for circulation; but no such note shall be for a sum less than five dollars, or for any sum which is not a multiple of five dollars, and the total amount of such notes, in circulation at any time, shall not exceed the amount of the unimpaired paid-up capital of the bank:

NOTE ISSUE OF BANQUE DU PEUPLE AND BANK OF BRITISH NORTH AMERICA.

2. Notwithstanding anything contained in the next preceding sub-section, the total amount of such notes in circulation at any time of La Banque du Peuple and the Bank of British North America respectively shall not exceed seventy-five per cent. of the unimpaired paid-up capital of such banks respectively, but each of such banks may issue such notes in excess of the said seventy-five per cent. upon depositing, with respect to such excess, with the Minister of Finance and Receiver General, in cash or bonds of the Dominion of Canada, an amount equal to the excess; provided always that in no case shall the total amount of the notes of either of the said banks in circulation at any time exceed the unimpaired paid-up capital of such bank; and the cash or bonds so deposited shall be available by the Minister of Finance and Receiver General for the redemption of notes issued in excess as aforesaid, in the event of the suspension of the said banks respectively:

PENALTIES FOR EXCESS OF CIRCULATION.

3. **If the total amount of the notes of the bank in circulation at any time exceeds the amount authorized by this section, the bank shall incur penalties as follows: If the amount of such excess is not over one thousand dollars, a penalty equal to the amount of such excess; if the amount of such excess is over one thousand dollars and is not over twenty thousand dollars, a penalty of one thousand dollars; if the amount of such excess is**

over twenty thousand dollars and is not over one hundred thousand dollars, a penalty of ten thousand dollars; if the amount of such excess is over one hundred thousand dollars and is not over two hundred thousand dollars, a penalty of fifty thousand dollars; and if the amount of such excess is over two hundred thousand dollars, a penalty of one hundred thousand dollars:

4. All notes heretofore issued or re-issued by the bank, and now in circulation, which are for a sum less than five dollars, or for a sum which is not a multiple of five dollars, shall be called in and cancelled as soon as practicable.

NOTES UNDER $5 TO BE CALLED IN.

52. The bank shall not pledge, assign, or hypothecate its notes; and no advance or loan made on the security of the notes of a bank shall be recoverable from the bank or its assets:

PLEDGING OF NOTES PROHIBITED.

2. Every person who, being the president, vice-president, director, principal partner *en commandite*, general manager, manager, cashier, or other officer of the bank, pledges, assigns, or hypothecates, or authorizes, or is concerned in the pledge, assignment or hypothecation of the notes of the bank, and every person who accepts, receives or takes, or authorizes or is concerned in the acceptance or receipt or taking of such notes as a pledge, assignment or hypothecation, shall be liable to a fine of not less than four hundred dollars and not more than two thousand dollars, or to imprisonment for not more than two years, or to both:

PENALTY FOR PLEDGING.

3. Every person who, being the president, vice-president, director, principal partner *en commandite*, general manager, manager, cashier, or other officer of a bank, with intent to defraud, issues or delivers, or authorizes or is concerned in the issue or delivery of notes of the bank intended for circulation and not then in circulation,—and every person who, with knowledge of such intent, accepts, receives or takes, or authorizes or is concerned in the acceptance, receipt or taking of such notes,—shall be guilty of a misdemeanor, and liable to imprisonment for a term not exceeding seven years, or to a fine not exceeding two thousand dollars, or to both.

PENALTY FOR IMPROPER ISSUE OR TAKING OF NOTES.

53. The payment of the notes issued or re-issued by the bank and intended for circulation, and then in circulation, together with any interest paid or payable thereon as hereinafter provided, shall be the first charge upon the assets of the bank in case of its insolvency; and the payment of any amount due to the Government of Canada, in trust or otherwise, shall be the second charge upon such assets; and the payment of any amount due to the government of any of the Provinces, in trust or otherwise, shall be the third charge upon such assets:

NOTES TO BE FIRST CHARGE ON ASSETS.

2. The amount of any penalties for which the bank is liable shall not form a charge upon the assets of such bank, in case of its insolvency, until all other liabilities are paid.

LIABILITY FOR PENALTIES IN CASE OF INSOLVENCY.

54. Every bank to which this Act applies, and which is carrying on its business at the time when this Act comes into force, shall, within fifteen days thereafter, pay to the Minister of Finance and Receiver General, a sum of money equal to two and one-half per cent. of the average amount of its notes in circulation during the twelve months next preceding the date of the coming into force of this Act, or if such bank has not been in operation for twelve months, a sum of money equal to two and one-half per cent. of the average amount of its notes in circulation during the time it has been in operation; and each bank shall, within fifteen days from and after the first day of July, in the year one thousand eight hundred and ninety-two, pay to the Minister of Finance and Receiver General such further sum of money as is necessary to make the total amount so paid by each bank to be a sum equal to five per cent. of the average amount of its notes in circulation during the twelve months next preceding the date last mentioned,—which sum shall be adjusted annually as hereinafter provided:

EXISTING BANKS TO MAKE DEPOSIT WITH MINISTER OF FINANCE EQUAL TO FIVE PER CENT. OF NOTE CIRCULATION.

2. The Merchants' Bank of Prince Edward Island shall, on or before the day upon which it becomes subject to the provisions of this Act, pay to the Minister of Finance and Receiver General such

sum as appears to the satisfaction of the Treasury Board to be equal to two and one-half per cent. of the average amount of its notes in circulation during the then preceding twelve months; and shall further pay to the Minister of Finance and Receiver General, within fifteen days from and after the first day of July in the year then next following, such further sum as is necessary to make the total sum paid by the said bank to be a sum equal to five per cent. of the average amount of its notes in circulation from the time the said bank became subject to the provisions of this Act to the said first day of July,—which sum shall be adjusted annually as hereinafter provided:

AS TO MERCHANTS' BANK OF P. E. I.

3. The Minister of Finance and Receiver General shall, upon the issue of a certificate under this Act authorizing a bank to issue notes and commence the business of banking, retain out of any moneys of such bank then in his possession the sum of five thousand dollars,—which sum shall be held for the purposes of this section, until the annual adjustment hereunder takes place in the year then next following, at which time the amount at the credit of the bank shall be adjusted by payment to or by the bank of such sum as is necessary to make the amount at the credit of the bank to be a sum of money equal to five per cent. of the average amount of its notes in circulation from the time it commenced business to the time of such adjustment,—which sum shall be adjusted annually as hereinafter provided:

AS TO NEW BANKS.

4. The amounts so paid, retained, and kept on deposit as aforesaid shall form a fund to be known as "The Bank Circulation Redemption Fund,"—which fund shall be held for the following purpose, and for no other, namely: In the event of the suspension by the bank of payment in specie or Dominion notes of any of its liabilities as they accrue, for the payment of the notes then issued or reissued by such bank, and intended for circulation, and then in circulation, and interest thereon; and the Minister of Finance and Receiver General shall, with respect to all notes paid out of the said fund, have the same rights as any other holder of the notes of the bank:

FORMATION OF CIRCULATION REDEMPTION FUND.

5. The fund shall bear interest at the rate of three per cent. per annum, and it shall be adjusted, as soon as possible after the thirtieth day of June in each year, in such a way as to make the amount at the credit of each bank contributing thereto, unless herein otherwise specially provided, equal to five per cent. of the average note circulation of such bank during the then next preceding twelve months:

FUND TO BEAR INTEREST.

6. The average note circulation of a bank during any period shall be determined from the average of the amount of its notes in circulation, as shown by the monthly returns for such period made by the bank to the Minister of Finance and Receiver General; and where, in any return, the greatest amount of notes in circulation at any time during the month is given, such amount shall, for the purposes of this section, be taken to be the amount of the notes of the bank in circulation during the month to which such return relates:

NOTE CIRCULATION, HOW DETERMINED.

7. In the event of the suspension by the bank of payment in specie or Dominion notes of any of its liabilities as they accrue, the notes of such bank, issued or reissued and intended for circulation, and then in circulation, shall bear interest at the rate of six per cent. per annum, from the day of such suspension to such day as is named by the directors, or by the liquidator, receiver, assignee or other proper official, for the payment thereof,—of which day notice shall be given by advertisement for at least three days in a newspaper published in the place in which the head office of the bank is situate; but in case any notes presented for payment on or after any day named for payment thereof are not paid, all notes then unpaid and in circulation shall continue to bear interest to such further day as is named for payment thereof,—of which day notice shall be given in manner above provided: Provided always, that in case of failure on the part of the directors of the bank, or of the liquidator, receiver, assignee or other proper official, to make arrangements within two months from the day of suspension of payment by the bank as aforesaid for the payment of all of its notes and interest thereon, the Minister of Finance and Receiver General

NOTES OF BANK SUSPENDING PAYMENT TO BEAR INTEREST UNTIL REDEEMED.

IF NOT REDEEMED TO BE PAID OUT OF FUND.

may thereupon make arrangements for the payment of the notes remaining unpaid, and all interest thereon, out of the said fund, and shall give such notice of such payment as he thinks expedient, and on the day named by him for such payment all interest on such notes shall cease, anything herein contained to the contrary notwithstanding; but nothing herein contained shall be construed to impose any liability on the Government of Canada or on the Minister of Finance and Receiver General beyond the amount available from time to time out of the said fund:

PROVISO.

8. All payments made from the said fund shall be without regard to the amount contributed thereto by the bank in respect of whose notes the payments are made; and in case the payments from the fund exceed the amount contributed by such bank to the fund, and all interest due or accruing due to such bank thereon, the other banks shall, on demand, make good to the fund the amount of such excess, *pro ratâ* to the amount which each bank has at that time contributed to the fund; and all amounts recovered and received by the Minister of Finance and Receiver General from the bank on whose account such payments were made shall, after the amount of such excess has been made good as aforesaid, be distributed among the banks contributing to make good such excess *pro ratâ* to the amount contributed by each: Provided always, that each of such other banks shall only be called upon to make good to the said fund its share of such excess, in payments not exceeding in any one year one per cent. of the average amount of its notes in circulation,—such circulation to be ascertained in such manner as the Minister of Finance and Receiver General decides; and his decision shall be final:

PAYMENTS FROM FUND TO BE WITHOUT REGARD TO AMOUNT CONTRIBUTED.

PROVISO.

9. In the event of the winding up of the business of a bank by reason of insolvency or otherwise, the Treasury Board may, on the application of the directors, or of the liquidator, receiver, assignee or other proper official, and on being satisfied that proper arrangements have been made for the payment of the notes of the bank and any interest thereon, pay over to such directors, liquidator, re-

REPAYMENT OF AMOUNT IF BANK IS WOUND UP.

ceiver, assignee or other proper official, the amount at the credit of the bank, or such portion thereof as it thinks expedient:

10. The Treasury Board may make all such rules and regulations as it thinks expedient with reference to the payment of any moneys out of the said fund, and the manner, place and time of such payments, the collection of all amounts due to the said fund, all accounts to be kept in connection therewith, and generally the management of the said fund and all matters relating thereto:

TREASURY BOARD MAY REGULATE MANAGEMENT OF FUND.

11. The Minister of Finance and Receiver General may, in his official name, by action in the Exchequer Court of Canada enforce payment (with costs of action) of any sum due and payable by any bank under the provisions of this section.

ENFORCEMENT OF PAYMENT.

55. The bank shall make such arrangements as are necessary to ensure the circulation at par in any and every part of Canada of all notes issued or reissued by it and intended for circulation; and towards this purpose the bank shall establish agencies for the redemption and payment of its notes at the cities of Halifax, St. John, Charlottetown, Montreal, Toronto, Winnipeg and Victoria, and at such other places as are, from time to time, designated by the Treasury Board.

NOTES OF BANK TO BE PAYABLE AT PAR THROUGHOUT CANADA.

56. The bank shall always receive in payment its own notes at par at any of its offices, and whether they are made payable there or not:

REDEMPTION OF NOTES.

2. The chief place of business of the bank shall always be one of the places at which its notes are made payable.

PAYABLE AT CHIEF PLACE OF BUSINESS.

57. The bank, when making any payment, shall, on the request of the person to whom the payment is to be made, pay the same, or such part thereof, not exceeding one hundred dollars, as such person requests, in Dominion notes for one, two, or four dollars each, at the

PAYMENTS IN DOMINION NOTES.

option of such person: Provided always, that no payment, whether in Dominion notes or bank notes, shall be made in bills that are torn or partially defaced by excessive handling.

TORN OR DEFACED NOTES.

58. The bonds, obligations and bills, obligatory or of credit, of the bank under its corporate seal, and signed by the president or vice-president, and countersigned by a cashier or assistant cashier, which are made payable to any person, shall be assignable by indorsement thereon; and bills or notes of the bank signed by the president, vice-president, cashier or other officer appointed by the directors of the bank to sign the same, promising the payment of money to any person or to his order, or to the bearer, though not under the corporate seal of the bank, shall be binding and obligatory on it in like manner and with the like force and effect as they would be upon any private person, if issued by him in his private or natural capacity, and shall be assignable in like manner as if they were so issued by a private person in his natural capacity: Provided always, that the directors of the bank may, from time to time, authorize, or depute any cashier, assistant cashier, or officer of the bank, or any director other than the president or vice-president, or any cashier, manager or local director of any branch or office of discount and deposit of the bank, to sign the notes of the bank intended for circulation.

BONDS, NOTES, ETC., HOW AND BY WHOM TO BE SIGNED.

PROVISO: POWER MAY BE DEPUTED TO OFFICER.

59. All bank notes and bills of the bank whereon the name of any person intrusted or authorized to sign such notes or bills on behalf of the bank is impressed by machinery provided for that purpose, by or with the authority of the bank, shall be good and valid to all intents and purposes as if such notes and bills had been subscribed in the proper handwriting of the person intrusted or authorized by the bank to sign the same respectively, and shall be bank notes and bills within the meaning of all laws and statutes whatever, and may be described as bank notes or bills in all indictments and civil or criminal proceedings whatsoever: Provided

NOTES MAY BE SIGNED BY MACHINERY.

ONE SIGNATURE MUST BE WRITTEN.

always, that at least one signature to each note or bill must be in the actual handwriting of a person authorized to sign such note or bill.

60. Every person, except a bank to which this Act applies, who issues or reissues, makes, draws, or endorses any bill, bond, note, cheque or other instrument, intended to circulate as money, or to be used as a substitute for money, for any amount whatsoever, shall incur a penalty of four hundred dollars, which shall be recoverable with costs, in any court of competent jurisdiction, by any person who sues for the same; and a moiety of such penalty shall belong to the person suing for the same, and the other moiety to Her Majesty for the public uses of Canada:

PENALTY FOR UNAUTHORIZED ISSUE OF NOTES FOR CIRCULATION.

2. The intention to pass any such instrument as money shall be presumed, if it is made for the payment of a less sum than twenty dollars, and is payable either in form or in fact to the bearer thereof, or at sight, or on demand, or at less than thirty days thereafter, or is overdue, or is in any way calculated or designed for circulation, or as a substitute for money; unless such instrument is a cheque on some chartered bank paid by the maker directly to his immediate creditor, or a promissory note, bill of exchange, bond or other undertaking for the payment of money, paid or delivered by the maker thereof to his immediate creditor, and is not designed to circulate as money or as a substitute for money.

WHAT SHALL BE DEEMED SUCH NOTES.

61. Every person who in any way defaces any Dominion or Provincial note, or bank note, whether by writing, printing, drawing or stamping thereon, or by attaching or affixing thereto, anything in the nature or form of an advertisement, shall be liable to a penalty not exceeding twenty dollars.

DEFACEMENT OF NOTES.

PENALTY.

62. Every officer charged with the receipt or disbursement of public moneys, and every officer of any bank, and every person acting as or employed by any banker, shall stamp or write in plain letters the word "counterfeit," "altered," or "worthless," upon every counter-

COUNTERFEIT AND FRAUDULENT NOTES TO BE STAMPED AS SUCH.

feit or fraudulent note issued in the form of a Dominion or bank note, and intended to circulate as money, which is presented to him at his place of business; and if such officer or person wrongfully stamps any genuine note he shall, upon presentation, redeem it at the face value thereof.

NO ADVERTISEMENT, ETC., TO BE ISSUED IN THE FORM OF A NOTE.

63. Every person who designs, engraves, prints or in any manner makes, executes, utters, issues, distributes, circulates or uses any business or professional card, notice, placard, circular, hand-bill or advertisement in the likeness or similitude of any Dominion or bank note, or any obligation or security of any Government, or of any bank, is liable to a penalty of one hundred dollars or to three months' imprisonment, or to both.

BUSINESS AND POWERS OF THE BANK.

BRANCHES AND AGENCIES.

GENERAL POWERS OF BANK.

CERTAIN BUSINESS MAY NOT BE TRANSACTED BY THE BANK.

64. The bank may open branches, agencies and offices, and may engage in and carry on business as a dealer in gold and silver coin and bullion, and it may deal in, discount, and lend money and make advances upon the security of, and may take as collateral security for any loan made by it, bills of exchange, promissory notes and other negotiable securities, or the stock, bonds, debentures and obligations of municipal and other corporations, whether secured by mortgage or otherwise, or Dominion, Provincial, British, foreign and other public securities, and it may engage in and carry on such business generally as appertains to the business of banking; but, except as authorized by this Act, it shall not, either directly or indirectly, deal in the buying, or selling, or bartering of goods, wares and merchandise, or engage or be engaged in any trade or business whatsoever; and it shall not, either directly or indirectly, purchase, or deal in, or lend money, or make advances upon the security or pledge of any share of its own capital stock, or of the capital stock of any bank; and it shall not, either directly or indirectly, lend money or make advances upon the security, mortgage, or hypothecation of any land, tenements, or immov-

able property, or of any ships or other vessels, or upon the security of any goods, wares and merchandise.

BANK TO HAVE LIEN ON DEBTOR'S SHARES.

SALE OF SUCH SHARES.

NOTICE.

TRANSFER IN CASE OF SALE.

65. The bank shall have a privileged lien, for any debt or liability for any debt to the bank, on the shares of its own capital stock and on any unpaid dividends of the debtor or person liable, and may decline to allow any transfer of the shares of such debtor or person until such debt is paid; and the bank shall, within twelve months after such debt has accrued and become payable, sell such shares, and notice shall be given to the holder thereof of the intention of the bank to sell the same, by mailing such notice in the post office to the last known address of such holder, at least thirty days prior to such sale; and upon such sale being made the president, vice-president, manager or cashier shall execute a transfer of such shares to the purchaser thereof in the usual transfer book of the bank, which transfer shall vest in such purchaser all the rights in or to such shares which were possessed by the holder thereof, with the same obligation of warranty on his part as if he were the vendor thereof, but without any warranty from the bank or by the officer of the bank executing such transfer.

COLLATERAL SECURITIES MAY BE SIMILARLY DEALT WITH.

66. The stock, bonds, debentures or securities, acquired and held by the bank as collateral security, may, in case of default to pay the debt, for securing which they were so acquired and held, be dealt with, sold and conveyed either in like manner and subject to the same restrictions as are herein provided in respect of stock of the bank on which it has acquired a lien under this Act, or in like manner as and subject to the restrictions under which a private individual might in like circumstances deal with, sell and convey the same, but without obligation to sell the same within twelve months:

RIGHT TO DO SO MAY BE WAIVED.

2. The right so to deal with and dispose of such stock, bonds, debentures or securities in manner aforesaid may be waived or varied by any agreement between the bank and the owner of such stock, bonds, debentures or securities,

made at the time at which such debt was incurred, or if the time of payment of such debt has been extended, then by an agreement made at the time of such extension.

67. The bank may acquire and hold real and immovable property for its actual use and occupation and the management of its business, and may sell or dispose of the same, and acquire other property in its stead for the same purpose.

REAL ESTATE FOR OCCUPATION.

68. The bank may take, hold and dispose of mortgages and *hypothèques* upon real or personal, immovable or movable property, by way of additional security for debts contracted to the bank in the course of its business; and the rights, powers and privileges which the bank is by this Act declared to have or to have had in respect of real or immovable property mortgaged to it, shall be held and possessed by it in respect of any personal or movable property which is mortgaged or hypothecated to it.

MORTGAGES AS ADDITIONAL SECURITY.

69. The bank may purchase any lands or real or immovable property offered for sale under execution, or in insolvency, or under the order or decree of a court, as belonging to any debtor to the bank, or offered for sale by a mortgagee or other encumbrancer having priority over a mortgage or other encumbrance held by the bank or offered for sale by the bank under a power of sale given to it for that purpose, in cases in which, under similar circumstances, an individual could so purchase, without any restriction as to the value of the property which it may so purchase, and may acquire a title thereto as any individual purchasing at sheriff's sale, or under a power of sale, in like circumstances, could do, and may take, have, hold and dispose of the same at pleasure.

PURCHASE OF LAND UNDER EXECUTION, ETC.

70. The bank may acquire and hold an absolute title in or to real or immovable property mortgaged to it as security for a debt due or owing to it, either by obtaining a release of the equity of redemption in the mortgaged property, or by procuring a foreclosure, or by other means whereby, as between individuals, an equity of redemp-

ABSOLUTE TITLE MAY BE ACQUIRED.

tion can, by law, be barred, and may purchase and acquire any prior mortgage or charge on such property: Provided always, that no bank shall hold any real or immovable property, howsoever acquired, except such as is required for its own use, for any period exceeding seven years from the date of the acquisition thereof.

PROVISO: SALE OF PROPERTY SO ACQUIRED.

71. Nothing in any charter, Act or law shall be construed as ever having prevented or as preventing the bank from acquiring and holding an absolute title to and in any such mortgaged real or immovable property, whatever the value thereof is, or from exercising or acting upon any power of sale contained in any mortgage given to it or held by it, authorizing or enabling it to sell or convey away any property so mortgaged.

TITLE TO LANDS SO ACQUIRED; POWER OF SALE, ETC.

72. Every bank advancing money in aid of the building of any ship or vessel shall have the same right of acquiring and holding security upon such ship or vessel, while building and when completed, either by way of mortgage, *hypothèque*, hypothecation, privilege, or lien thereon, or purchase or transfer thereof, as individuals have in the Province wherein such ship or vessel is being built, and for that purpose may avail itself of all such rights and means of obtaining and enforcing such security, and shall be subject to all such obligations, limitations and conditions as are, by the law of such Province, conferred or imposed upon individuals making such advances.

AS TO ADVANCES FOR BUILDING SHIPS.

73. The bank may acquire and hold any warehouse receipt or bill of lading as collateral security for the payment of any debt incurred in its favor in the course of its banking business; and the warehouse receipt or bill of lading so acquired shall vest in the bank, from the date of the acquisition thereof, all the right and title of the previous holder or owner thereof, or of the person from whom such goods, wares and merchandise were received or acquired by the bank, if the warehouse receipt or bill of lading is made directly in favor of the

WAREHOUSE RECEIPTS MAY BE TAKEN AS COLLATERAL SECURITY.

bank, instead of to the previous holder or owner of such goods, wares and merchandise:

2. If the previous holder of such warehouse receipt or bill of lading is the agent of the owner of the goods, wares and merchandise mentioned therein, the bank shall be vested with all the right and title of the owner thereof, subject to his right to have the same re-transferred to him, if the debt, as security for which they are held by the bank, is paid:

WHEN PREVIOUS HOLDER IS AN AGENT.

3. In this section the expression "agent" means any person intrusted with the possession of goods, wares and merchandise, or to whom the same are consigned, or who is possessed of any bill of lading, receipt, order, or other document used in the course of business as proof of the possession or control of goods, wares and merchandise, or authorizing or purporting to authorize, either by indorsement or by delivery, the possessor of such document to transfer or receive the goods, wares and merchandise thereby represented; and such person shall be deemed the possessor of such goods, wares and merchandise, bill of lading, receipt, order, or other document as aforesaid, as well if the same are held by any person for him or subject to his control as if he is in actual possession thereof.

INTERPRETATION OF "AGENT."

74. The bank may lend money to any person engaged in business as a wholesale manufacturer of any goods, wares and merchandise, upon the security of the goods, wares and merchandise manufactured by him or procured for such manufacture:

LOANS TO WHOLESALE MANUFACTURERS.

2. The bank may also lend money to any wholesale purchaser or shipper of products of agriculture, the forest and mine, or the sea, lakes and rivers, or to any wholesale purchaser or shipper of live stock or dead stock, and the products thereof, upon the security of such products, or of such live stock or dead stock, and the products thereof:

LOANS TO CERTAIN WHOLESALE PURCHASERS OR SHIPPERS.

3. Such security may be given by the owner and may be taken

in the form set forth in Schedule C to this Act, or to the like effect; and by virtue of such security, the bank shall acquire the same rights and powers in respect to the goods, wares and merchandise, stock or products covered thereby, as if it had acquired the same by virtue of a warehouse receipt.

FORM OF SECURITY.

75. The bank shall not acquire or hold any warehouse receipt or bill of lading or security under the next preceding section to secure the payment of any bill, note or debt, unless such bill, note or debt is negotiated or contracted at the time of the acquisition thereof by the bank, or upon the written promise or agreement that such warehouse receipt or bill of lading or security would be given to the bank; but such bill, note or debt may be renewed, or the time for the payment thereof extended, without affecting any such security:

WHEN SUCH SECURITY MAY BE ACQUIRED.

2. The bank may, on shipment of any goods, wares and merchandise for which it holds a warehouse receipt, or security as aforesaid, surrender such receipt or security and receive a bill of lading in exchange therefor, or, on the receipt of any goods, wares and merchandise for which it holds a bill of lading or security, as aforesaid, it may surrender such bill of lading or security, store such goods, wares and merchandise, and take a warehouse receipt therefor, or may ship them, or part of them, and take another bill of lading therefor:

EXCHANGE OF WAREHOUSE RECEIPT FOR BILL OF LADING AND *vice versâ*.

3. Every one is guilty of a misdemeanor and liable to imprisonment for a term not exceeding two years who wilfully makes any false statement in any warehouse receipt, bill of lading or security, as aforesaid.

PENALTY FOR MAKING FALSE STATEMENT.

4. Every one is guilty of a misdemeanor and liable to imprisonment for a term not exceeding two years, who, having possession or control of any goods, wares and merchandise covered by any warehouse receipt, bill of lading or security as aforesaid, and having knowledge of such receipt, bill of lading or security, and without consent of the bank, in writing and before the advance, bill, note or debt thereby secured

PENALTY FOR ALIENATING GOODS SO SECURED.

has been fully paid, wilfully alienates or parts with any such goods, wares, or merchandise, or wilfully withholds from the bank possession thereof upon demand after default in payment of such advance, bill, note or debt.

AS TO GOODS MANUFACTURED FROM ARTICLES PLEDGED.

76. If goods, wares and merchandise are manufactured or produced from the goods, wares and merchandise, or any of them, included in or covered by any warehouse receipt, or security given under section seventy-four of this Act, while so covered, the bank holding such warehouse receipt or security shall hold or continue to hold such goods, wares and merchandise, during the process and after the completion of such manufacture or production, with the same right and title and for the same purposes and upon the same conditions as it held or could have held the original goods, wares and merchandise.

PRIOR CLAIM OF THE BANK OVER UNPAID VENDOR.

77. All advances made on the security of any bill of lading or warehouse receipt, or security given under section seventy-four of this Act, shall give to the bank making such advances a claim for the repayment of such advances on the goods, wares and merchandise therein mentioned, or into which they have been converted, prior to and by preference over the claim of any unpaid vendor; but such preference shall not be given over the claim of any unpaid vendor who had a lien upon such goods, wares and merchandise at the time of the acquisition by the bank of such warehouse receipt, bill of lading, or security, unless the same was acquired without knowledge on the part of the bank of such lien.

SALE OF GOODS ON NON-PAYMENT OF DEBT.

78. In the event of the non-payment at maturity of any debt secured by a warehouse receipt or bill of lading, or security given under section seventy-four of this Act, the bank may sell the goods, wares and merchandise mentioned therein, or so much thereof as will suffice to pay such debt with interest and expenses, returning the overplus, if any, to the person from whom such warehouse receipt, or bill of lading, or security, or the goods, wares and merchandise mentioned therein, as the case may be, were acquired; but such power of sale shall be subject to the following provisions, namely:

2. No sale without the consent in writing of the owner of any timber, boards, deals, staves, saw-logs or other lumber, shall be made under this Act until notice of the time and place of such sale has been given by a registered letter, mailed in the post office to the last known address of the pledger thereof, at least thirty days prior to the sale thereof; and no goods, wares and merchandise, other than timber, boards, deals, staves, saw-logs or other lumber, shall be sold by the bank under this Act without the consent of the owner, until notice of the time and place of sale has been given by a registered letter, mailed in the post office to the last known address of the pledger thereof, at least ten days prior to the sale thereof:

NOTICE TO BE GIVEN BEFORE SALE OF GOODS PLEDGED.

3. Every such sale of any article mentioned in this section, without the consent of the owner, shall be made by public auction, after a notice thereof by advertisement, stating the time and place thereof, in at least two newspapers published in or nearest to the place where the sale is to be made; and if such sale is in the Province of Quebec, then at least one of such newspapers shall be a newspaper published in the English language, and one other such newspaper shall be a newspaper published in the French language.

SALE BY AUCTION AFTER NOTICE.

79. Every bank which violates any provision contained in any of the sections numbered sixty-four to seventy-eight (both inclusive) shall incur for each violation thereof a penalty not exceeding five hundred dollars.

PENALTY FOR CONTRAVENTION.

80. The bank shall not be liable to incur any penalty or forfeiture for usury, and may stipulate for, take, reserve or exact any rate of interest or discount not exceeding seven per cent. per annum, and may receive and take in advance any such rate, but no higher rate of interest shall be recoverable by the bank; and the bank may allow any rate of interest whatever upon money deposited with it.

NO PENALTY FOR USURY.

WHAT INTEREST MAY BE ALLOWED.

81. No promissory note, bill of exchange or other negotiable security, discounted by or indorsed or otherwise assigned to the bank, shall be held to be void, usurious or tainted by usury, as regards such bank, or any maker, drawer, acceptor, indorser, or indorsee thereof, or other party thereto, or *bonâ fide* holder thereof, nor shall any party thereto be subject to any penalty or forfeiture by reason of any rate of interest taken, stipulated or received by such bank, on or with respect to such promissory note, bill of exchange, or other negotiable security, or paid or allowed by any party thereto to another in compensation for, or in consideration of the rate of interest taken or to be taken thereon by such bank; but no party thereto, other than the bank, shall be entitled to recover or liable to pay more than the lawful rate of interest in the Province where the suit is brought, nor shall the bank be entitled to recover a higher rate than seven per cent. per annum; and no innocent holder of or party to any promissory note, bill of exchange or other negotiable security, shall, in any case be deprived of any remedy against any party thereto, or liable to any penalty or forfeiture, by reason of any usury or offence against the laws of any such Province, respecting interest, committed in respect of such note, bill or negotiable security, without the complicity or consent of such innocent holder or party.

NO INSTRUMENT TO BE VOID ON GROUND OF USURY.

AS TO INNOCENT HOLDERS.

82. The bank may, in discounting at any of its places of business, branches, agencies or offices of discount and deposit, any note, bill or other negotiable security or paper payable at any other of its own places or seats of business, branches, agencies or offices of discount and deposit in Canada, receive or retain, in addition to the discount, any amount not exceeding the following rates per cent. according to the time it has to run, on the amount of such note, bill or other negotiable security or paper, to defray the expenses attending the collection thereof, that is to say: under thirty days, one-eighth of one per cent.; thirty days or over, but under sixty days, one-fourth of one per cent.;

COLLECTION FEES.

sixty days and over, but under ninety days, three-eights of one per cent.; ninety days and over, one-half of one per cent.

AGENCY FEES.

83. The bank may, in discounting any note, bill or other negotiable security or paper, *boná fide* payable at any place in Canada different from that at which it is discounted, and other than one of its own places or seats of business, branches, agencies or offices of discount and deposit in Canada, receive and retain, in addition to the discount thereon, a sum not exceeding one-half of one per cent. on the amount thereof, to defray the expenses of agency and charges in collecting the same.

DEPOSITS MAY BE RECEIVED FROM PERSONS UNABLE TO CONTRACT.

84. The bank may receive deposits from any person whomsoever, whatever his age, status or condition in life, and whether such person is qualified by law to enter into ordinary contracts or not; and, from time to time, may repay any or all of the principal thereof, and may pay the whole or any part of the interest thereon to such person, without the authority, aid, assistance or intervention of any person or official being required, unless before such repayment the money so deposited in and repaid by the bank is lawfully claimed as the property of some other person, in which case it may be paid to the depositor with the consent of the claimant, or to the claimant with the consent of the depositor: Provided always, that if the person making any such deposit could not, under the law of the Province where the deposit is made, deposit and withdraw money in and from a bank without this section, the total amount to be received from such person on deposit shall not, at any time, exceed the sum of five hundred dollars:

PROVISO: AMOUNT LIMITED.

BANK NOT BOUND TO SEE TO TRUSTS IN RELATION TO SUCH DEPOSITS.

2. The bank shall not be bound to see to the execution of any trust, whether expressed, implied or constructive, to which any deposit made under the authority of this section is subject; and except only in the case of a lawful claim, by some other person before repayment, the receipt of the person in whose name any such deposit stands, or if it stands in the name of two persons the receipt of

one, or if in the names of more than two persons the receipt of a majority of such persons, shall be a sufficient discharge to all concerned for the payment of any money payable in respect of such deposit, notwithstanding any trust to which such deposit is then subject, and whether or not the bank sought to be charged with such trust (and with whom the deposit has been made) had notice thereof; and the bank shall not be bound to see to the application of the money paid upon such receipt.

RETURNS BY THE BANK.

85. Monthly returns shall be made by the bank to the Minister of Finance and Receiver General in the form set forth in Schedule D to this Act, and shall be made up and sent in within the first fifteen days of each month, and shall exhibit the condition of the bank on the last juridical day of the month next preceding; and such monthly returns shall be signed by the chief accountant and by the president, or vice-president, or the director or principal partner then acting as president, and by the manager, cashier or other principal officer of the bank at its chief place of business:

MONTHLY RETURNS TO GOVERNMENT.

2. Every bank which neglects to make up and send in, as aforesaid, any monthly return required by this section within the time hereby limited, shall incur a penalty of fifty dollars for each and every day after the expiration of such time during which the bank neglects so to make up and send in such return; and the date upon which it appears by the post office stamp or mark upon the envelope or wrapper enclosing such return for transmission to the Minister of Finance and Receiver General, that the same was deposited in the post office, shall be taken *primâ facie*, for the purposes of this section, to be the date upon which such return was made up and sent in.

PENALTY FOR NOT MAKING UP MONTHLY RETURNS IN DUE TIME.

86. The Minister of Finance and Receiver General may also call for special returns from any bank, whenever, in his judgment, they are necessary to afford a full and complete knowledge of its condition:

SPECIAL RETURNS MAY BE CALLED FOR.

2. Such special returns shall be made and signed in the manner and by the persons specified in the next preceding section, and every bank which neglects to make and send in any such special return within thirty days from the date of the demand therefor by the Minister of Finance and Receiver General shall incur a penalty of five hundred dollars for each and every day such neglect continues; and the provisions contained in the last preceding section as to the *primâ facie* evidence of the date upon which returns are made up and sent in thereunder, shall apply to returns made under this section: Provided always, that the Minister of Finance and Receiver General may extend the time for sending in such special returns for such further period, not exceeding thirty days, as he thinks expedient.

PENALTY FOR NOT MAKING SUCH RETURN IN DUE TIME.

87. The bank shall, within twenty days after the close of each calendar year, transmit or deliver to the Minister of Finance and Receiver General, to be by him laid before Parliament, a certified list showing the names of the shareholders of the bank on the last day of such calendar year, with their additions and residences, the number of shares then held by them respectively, and the value at par of such shares:

TRANSMISSION OF CERTIFIED LISTS OF SHAREHOLDERS TO MINISTER OF FINANCE.

2. Such list shall be delivered at the Department of Finance, or shall be sent by registered letter posted at such time that, in the ordinary course of post, it may be delivered at the said Department within the time above limited:

MODE OF TRANSMISSION.

3. Every bank which neglects to transmit such list in manner aforesaid within the time aforesaid shall incur a penalty of fifty dollars for each and every day during which such neglect continues.

PENALTY FOR NEGLECT TO TRANSMIT SUCH LISTS.

88. The bank shall, within twenty days after the close of each calendar year, transmit or deliver to the Minister of Finance and Receiver General, to be by him laid before Parliament, a return of all dividends which have remained unpaid for more than five years, and also of all amounts or balances in respect to which no transactions have

ANNUAL STATEMENT OF DIVIDENDS REMAINING UNPAID, ETC.

taken place or upon which no interest has been paid during the five years prior to the date of such return: Provided always, that in case of moneys deposited for a fixed period, the period of five years above referred to shall be reckoned from the date of the termination of such fixed period: PROVISO.

2. Such return shall be signed in the manner required for the monthly returns under section eighty-five of this Act, and shall set forth the name of each shareholder or creditor, his last known address, the amount due, the agency of the bank at which the last transaction took place, and the date thereof; and if such shareholder or creditor is known to the bank to be dead, such return shall show the names and addresses of his legal representatives, so far as known to the bank: DETAILS OF RETURN. FURTHER DETAILS.

3. Every bank which neglects to transmit or deliver to the Minister of Finance and Receiver General the return above referred to, within the time hereinbefore limited, shall incur a penalty of fifty dollars for each and every day during which such neglect continues: PENALTY FOR NOT MAKING ANNUAL RETURN.

4. If, in the event of the winding up of the business of the bank in insolvency, or under any general winding-up Act, or otherwise, any moneys payable by the liquidator, either to shareholders or depositors, remain unclaimed for the period of three years from the date of suspension of payment by the bank, or from the commencement of the winding up of such business, or until the final winding up of such business, if such takes place before the expiration of the said three years, such moneys and all interest thereon shall, notwithstanding any statute of limitations or other Act relating to prescription, be paid to the Minister of Finance and Receiver General, to be held by him subject to all rightful claims on behalf of any person other than the bank; and in case a claim to any moneys so paid as aforesaid is thereafter established to the satisfaction of the Treasury Board, the Governor in Council shall, on the report of the Treasury Board, direct payment thereof to be made to the person entitled thereto, together with interest on the principal sum thereof at the rate of three per cent. per DISPOSAL OF UNCLAIMED MONEYS.

annum for a period not exceeding six years from the date of payment thereof to the said Minister of Finance and Receiver General as aforesaid: Provided however, that no such interest shall be paid or payable on such principal sum, unless interest thereon was payable by the bank paying the same to the said Minister of Finance and Receiver General: Provided also, that on payment to the Minister of Finance and Receiver General as herein provided, the bank and its assets shall be held to be discharged from further liability for the amounts so paid.

PROVISO.

PROVISO.

5. Upon the winding up of a bank in insolvency or under any general winding-up Act, or otherwise, the assignees, liquidators, directors or other officials in charge of such winding up, shall, before the final distribution of the assets, or within three years from the commencement of the suspension of payment by the bank, whichever shall first happen, pay over to the Minister of Finance and Receiver General a sum out of the assets of the bank equal to the amount then outstanding of the notes intended for circulation issued by the bank; and, upon such payment being made, the bank and its assets shall be relieved from all further liability in respect of such outstanding notes. The sum so paid shall be held by the Minister of Finance and Receiver General and applied for the purpose of redeeming, whenever presented, such outstanding notes, without interest.

REQUIREMENTS AS TO OUTSTANDING NOTES IN CASE OF INSOLVENCY.

INSOLVENCY.

89. In the event of the property and assets of the bank being insufficient to pay its debts and liabilities, each shareholder of the bank shall be liable for the deficiency to an amount equal to the par value of the shares held by him, in addition to any amount not paid up on such shares.

LIABILITY OF SHAREHOLDERS IN CASE OF INSUFFICIENCY OF ASSETS.

90. As a condition of the rights and privileges conferred by this Act or by any Act in amendment thereof, the following provision

shall have effect:—The liability of the bank under any law, custom, or agreement to repay moneys deposited with it and interest (if any) and to pay dividends declared and payable on its capital stock, shall continue notwithstanding any statute of limitations or any enactment or law relating to prescription: PROVISION AS TO PRESCRIPTION AND STATUTE OF LIMITATIONS.

2. This section applies to moneys heretofore or hereafter deposited, and to dividends heretofore or hereafter declared. RETROACTION.

91. Any suspension by the bank of payment of any of its liabilities as they accrue, in specie or Dominion notes, shall, if it continues for ninety days, consecutively, or at intervals within twelve consecutive months, constitute the bank insolvent and operate a forfeiture of its charter or Act of incorporation, so far as regards all further banking operations; and the charter or Act of incorporation shall remain in force only for the purpose of enabling the directors or other lawful authority to make and enforce the calls mentioned in the next following sections of this Act and to wind up its business. SUSPENSION FOR 90 DAYS TO CONSTITUTE INSOLVENCY.

92. If any suspension of payment in full in specie or Dominion notes of all or any of the notes or other liabilities of the bank continues for three months after the expiration of the time which, under the preceding section, would constitute the bank insolvent, and if no proceedings are taken under any general or special Act for the winding up of the bank, the directors shall make calls on the shareholders thereof, to the amount they deem necessary to pay all the debts and liabilities of the bank, without waiting for the collection of any debts due to it or the sale of any of its assets or property: CALLS IN SUCH CASES.

2. Such calls shall be made at intervals of thirty days, and upon notice to be given thirty days at least prior to the day on which such call shall be payable, and any number of such calls may be made by one resolution; any such call shall not exceed twenty per cent. on each share; and payment of such calls may be enforced in like manner as payment of calls on HOW SUCH CALLS SHALL BE MADE AND ENFORCED.

unpaid stock may be enforced; and the first of such calls may be made within ten days after the expiration of the said three months:

3. Every director who refuses to make or enforce, or to concur in making or enforcing any call under this section, is guilty of a misdemeanor, and liable to imprisonment for any term not exceeding two years, and shall further be personally responsible for any damages suffered by such default.

REFUSAL TO MAKE CALLS UNDER THIS SECTION A MISDEMEANOR.

93. In the event of proceedings being taken under any general or special winding-up Act, in consequence of the insolvency of the bank, the said calls shall be made in the manner prescribed for the making of such calls in such general or special winding-up Act.

CALLS UNDER WINDING-UP ACT.

94. Any failure on the part of any shareholder liable to any such call to pay the same when due, shall operate a forfeiture by such shareholder of all claim in or to any part of the assets of the bank,—such call and any further call thereafter being nevertheless recoverable from him as if no such forfeiture had been incurred.

FORFEITURE FOR NON-PAYMENT.

95. Nothing in the six sections next preceding contained shall be construed to alter or diminish the additional liabilities of the directors as hereinbefore mentioned and declared.

LIABILITY OF DIRECTORS NOT DIMINISHED.

96. Persons who, having been shareholders of the bank, have only transferred their shares, or any of them, to others, or registered the transfer thereof within sixty days before the commencement of the suspension of payment by the bank, and persons whose subscriptions to the stock of the bank have been cancelled in manner hereinbefore provided within the said period of sixty days before the commencement of the suspension of payment by the bank, shall be liable to all calls on the shares held or subscribed for by them, as if they held such shares at the time of such suspension of payment, saving their recourse against those by whom such shares were then actually held.

LIABILITY OF SHAREHOLDERS WHO HAVE TRANSFERRED THEIR STOCK.

OFFENCES AND PENALTIES.

97. Every one is guilty of a misdemeanor and liable to imprisonment for a term not exceeding two years who, being the president, vice-president, director, principal partner *en commandite*, manager, cashier or other officer of the bank, wilfully gives or concurs in giving any creditor of the bank any fraudulent, undue or unfair preference over other creditors, by giving security to such creditor or by changing the nature of his claim or otherwise howsoever, and shall further be responsible for all damages sustained by any person in consequence of such preference.

PRESIDENT, ETC., GIVING UNDUE PREFERENCE TO ANY CREDITOR, GUILTY OF A MISDEMEANOR.

98. The amount of all penalties imposed upon a bank for any violation of this Act shall be recoverable and enforceable with costs, at the suit of Her Majesty, instituted by the Attorney General of Canada, or the Minister of Finance and Receiver General, and such penalties shall belong to the Crown for the public uses of Canada; but the Governor in Council, on the report of the Treasury Board, may direct that any portion of any penalty be remitted or paid to any person, or applied in any manner deemed best adapted to attain the objects of this Act and to secure the due administration thereof.

RECOVERY AND DISPOSAL OF PENALTIES.

99. The making of any wilfully false or deceptive statement in any account, statement, return, report or other document respecting the affairs of the bank, is, unless it amounts to a higher offence, a misdemeanor punishable by imprisonment for a term not exceeding five years; and every president, vice-president, director, principal partner *en commandite*, auditor, manager, cashier or other officer of the bank, who prepares, signs, approves or concurs in such statement, return, report or document, or uses the same with intent to deceive or mislead any person, shall be held to have wilfully made such false statement, and shall further be responsible for all damages sustained by any person in consequence thereof.

MAKING FALSE STATEMENT IN RETURNS, ETC., A MISDEMEANOR, ETC.

UNAUTHORIZED USE OF TITLE "BANK," ETC.

100. Every person assuming or using the title of "bank," "banking company," "banking house," "banking association," or "banking institution," without being authorized so to do by this Act, or by some other Act in force in that behalf, is guilty of an offence against this Act.

PENALTY FOR OFFENCE AGAINST THIS ACT.

101. Every person, committing an offence declared to be an offence against this Act, shall be liable to a fine not exceeding one thousand dollars, or to imprisonment for a term not exceeding five years, or to both, in the discretion of the court before which the conviction is had.

PUBLIC NOTICES.

HOW NOTICES SHALL BE GIVEN.

102. The several public notices by this Act required to be given shall, unless otherwise specified, be given by advertisement in one or more newspapers published at the place where the head office of the bank is situate, and in the *Canada Gazette.*

DOMINION GOVERNMENT CHEQUES.

GOVERNMENT CHEQUES TO BE PAID AT PAR.

103. The bank shall not charge any discount or commission for cashing any official cheque of the Government of Canada, or of any department thereof, whether drawn on itself or on another bank.

COMMENCEMENT OF ACT AND REPEAL.

COMMENCEMENT OF THIS ACT.

REPEAL OF R. S. C., c. 120 AND OF 51 V., c. 27 AND 50-51 V., c. 47.

104. This Act shall come into force on the first day of July, in the year one thousand eight hundred and ninety-one; and from that day chapter one hundred and twenty of the Revised Statutes of Canada, intituled "*An Act respecting Banks and Banking*," the Act passed in the fifty-first year of Her Majesty's reign, chapter twenty-seven, in amendment thereof, the Act passed in the session held in the thirty-third year of Her Majesty's reign, chapter twelve, intituled "*An Act to remove certain restrictions with respect to the issue of bank notes in Nova Scotia*," the

Act passed in the session held in the fiftieth and fifty-first years of Her Majesty's reign, chapter forty-seven, intituled "*An Act respecting the defacing of counterfeit notes, and the use of imitations of notes,*" and chapter one hundred and twenty of the Revised Statutes of New Brunswick, "*Of Banking,*" and the Act passed by the Legislature of the Province of New Brunswick in the nineteenth year of Her Majesty's reign, chapter forty-seven, intituled "*An Act to explain chapter 120, Title XXXI, of the Revised Statutes, 'Of Banking,'*" shall be repealed, except as to rights theretofore acquired or liabilities incurred in regard to any matter or thing done or contract or agreement made or entered into or offences committed under the said chapters or Acts, and nothing in this Act shall effect any action or proceedings then pending under the said chapter or Acts then repealed, but the same shall be decided as if such chapters and Acts had not been repealed.

SAVING CLAUSE.

SCHEDULE A.

BANKS WHOSE CHARTERS ARE CONTINUED BY THIS ACT.

1. The Bank of Montreal.
2. The Quebec Bank.
3. La Banque du Peuple.
4. The Molsons Bank.
5. The Bank of Toronto.
6. The Ontario Bank.
7. The Eastern Townships Bank.
8. La Banque Nationale.
9. La Banque Jacques Cartier.
10. The Merchants' Bank of Canada.
11. The Union Bank of Canada.
12. The Canadian Bank of Commerce.
13. The Dominion Bank.
14. The Merchants' Bank of Halifax.

15. The Bank of Nova Scotia.
16. The Bank of Yarmouth.
17. La Banque Ville Marie.
18. The Standard Bank of Canada.
19. The Bank of Hamilton.
20. The Halifax Banking Company.
21. La Banque d'Hochelaga.
22. The Imperial Bank of Canada.
23. La Banque de St. Hyacinthe.
24. The Bank of Ottawa.
25. The Bank of New Brunswick.
26. The Exchange Bank of Yarmouth.
27. The Union Bank of Halifax.
28. The People's Bank of Halifax.
29. La Banque de St. Jean.
30. The Commercial Bank of Windsor.
31. The Western Bank of Canada.
32. The Commercial Bank of Manitoba.
33. The Traders' Bank of Canada.
34. The People's Bank of New Brunswick.
35. The Saint Stephen's Bank.
36. The Summerside Bank.

SCHEDULE B

FORM OF ACT OF INCORPORATION OF NEW BANKS.

An Act to incorporate the   Bank.

Whereas the persons hereinafter named have, by their petition, prayed that an Act be passed for the purpose of establishing a bank in   , and it is expedient to grant the prayer of the said petition :

Therefore Her Majesty, by and with the advice and consent of the Senate and House of Commons of Canada, enacts as follows :—

1. The persons hereinafter named, together with such others as

become shareholders in the corporation by this Act created, are hereby constituted a corporation by the name of hereinafter called "the Bank."

2. The capital stock of the bank shall be dollars.

3. The chief office of the bank shall be at

4. shall be the provisional directors of the bank.

5. This Act shall, subject to the provisions of section sixteen of "The Bank Act," remain in force until the first day of July, in the year one thousand nine hundred and one.

SCHEDULE C.

FORM OF SECURITY UNDER SECTION SEVENTY-FOUR.

In consideration of an advance of dollars, made by the (*name of bank*) to A. B., for which the said bank holds the following bills or notes (*describe fully the notes or bills held, if any*), the goods, wares and merchandise mentioned below are hereby assigned to the said bank as security for the payment, on or before the day of of the said advance, together with interest thereon at the rate of per cent. per annum from the day of (*or*, of the said bills and notes, or renewals thereof, or substitutions therefor, and interest thereon, *or as the case may be*).

This security is given under the provisions of section seventy-four of "The Bank Act," and is subject to all the provisions of the said Act.

The said goods, wares and merchandise are now owned by and are now in possession, and are free from any mortgage, lien or charge thereon (*or as the case may be*), and are in (*place or places where goods are*), and are the following: (*particular description of goods assigned*).

Dated at 18 .

SCHEDULE D.

Return of the liabilities and assets of the bank on the day of , A. D.

Capital authorized . . . . . $
Capital subscribed . . . . . $
Capital paid up . . . . . . $
Amount of rest or reserve fund . $
Rate per cent. of last dividend declared. per cent.

LIABILITIES.

1. Notes in circulation . . . $
2. Balance due to Dominion Government, after deducting advances for credits, pay-lists, etc . . .
3. Balance due to Provincial Governments . . . .
4. Deposits by the public, payable on demand . . . .
5. Deposits by the public, payable after notice or on a fixed day . . .
6. Loans from other banks in Canada, secured . . . .
7. Deposits, payable on demand or after notice or on a fixed day, made by other banks in Canada . . .
8. Balances due to other banks in Canada in daily exchanges . . .
9. Balances due to agencies of the bank, or to other banks or agencies in foreign countries . . . . .
10. Balances due to agencies of the bank, or to other banks or agencies in the United Kingdom . . .
11. Liabilities not included under foregoing heads . . . .

$

ASSETS.

1. Specie . . . . $
2. Dominion notes . . . .
3. Deposits with Dominion Government for security of note circulation .
4. Notes of and cheques on other banks.
5. Loans to other banks in Canada, secured . . . .
6. Deposits, payable on demand or after notice or on a fixed day, made with other banks in Canada . . .
7. Balances due from other banks in Canada in daily exchanges . .
8. Balances due from agencies of the bank, or from other banks or agencies in foreign countries . . .
9. Balances due from agencies of the bank, or from other banks or agencies in the United Kingdom . .
10. Dominion Government debentures or stocks . . . .
11. Canadian municipal securities, and British, Provincial, or foreign, or colonial public securities, (other than Dominion) . . . .
12. Canadian British and other railway securities . . . .
13. Call loans on bonds and stocks . .
14. Current loans . . . .
15. Loans to the Government of Canada .
16. Loans to Provincial Governments .
17. Overdue debts . . . . . .
18. Real estate, the property of the bank (other than the bank premises) .
19. Mortgages on real estate sold by the bank. . . . .
20. Bank premises . . . . . .
21. Other assets not included under the foregoing heads . . . . .

$

Aggregate amount of loans to directors, and firms of which they are partners, $

Average amount of specie held during the month, $

Average amount of Dominion notes held during the month, $

Greatest amount of notes in circulation at any time during the month, $

I declare that the above return has been prepared under my directions and is correct according to the books of the bank.

E. F.,

Chief Accountant.

We declare that the foregoing return is made up from the books of the bank, and that to the best of our knowledge and belief it is correct, and shows truly and clearly the financial position of the bank; and we further declare that the bank has never, at any time during the period to which the said return relates, held less than forty per cent. of its cash reserves in Dominion notes.

(*Place*) this day of

A. B., *President.*

C. D., *General Manager.*

MEMORANDA.

The currency of Canada is in dollars, cents, and mills, at the rate of 10 mills for a cent and 100 cents for a dollar. The British sovereign is legal tender for $4.86⅔.

Silver coin minted for circulation in Canada by order of Queen Victoria, is legal tender to the amount of ten dollars, and copper coin to the amount of twenty-five cents. The gold eagle of the United States is legal tender for ten dollars. Canada has no gold coinage of her own.

The Government of Canada and the chartered banks only are authorized to issue paper money. The Government currency is issued in denominations of four dollars, two dollars, one dollar, and twenty-five cents; no bank being permitted to issue notes for less sum than five dollars, or for any sum not a multiple of five dollars. The Dominion note issue is limited to $21,000,000.

$11,000,000 of the Dominion note circulation are in notes of $500 and $1,000, and are principally held by the banks as part of their cash reserve.

In order to secure the redemption of Dominion Government notes, the Minister of Finance is required to hold in gold and securities guaranteed by the Imperial Government, a sum equal to 25 per cent. of the amount issued, of which 15 per cent. must be in gold and 10 per cent. in guaranteed securities—the remaining 75 per cent. to be covered by Dominion debentures, issued by authority of Parliament.

The development of banking business in Canada is seen from the following statement:

	Capital Paid Up, Per Head of Population.	Circulation Per Head.	People's Deposits Per Head.	People's Discounts Per Head.	Liabilities.	Assets.
1871	$10.30	$5.75	$15.48	$23.33	$22.07	$34.46
1881	13.76	6.60	21.81	27.04	29.40	46.38
1891	12.56	6.54	30.70	35.40	38.75	55.72

In addition to the capital paid up in 1891, the reserve fund of the banks in that year amounted to $4.72 per head of population.

The first chartered bank to suspend business since Confederation (1867) was the Commercial Bank of New Brunswick. The Bank of Acadia (Liverpool, N. S.), suspended in 1873; the Metropolitan Bank of Montreal in 1877; the Mechanics' Bank of Montreal, the Consolidated Bank of Montreal, the Bank of Liverpool, N. S., and the Stadacona Bank of Quebec, in 1879; the Exchange Bank of Canada, in 1883; the Maritime Bank, of St. John, N. B., the Pictou Bank, the Bank of London, Ont., and the Central Bank of Canada retired from business in 1887, and the Federal Bank in 1888; the Commercial Bank of Manitoba closed its doors in 1893. In all, fourteen banks have suspended, representing assets of over $22,000,000, and liabilities of over $15,000,000.

The Commercial Bank of Manitoba failed in July, 1893. The notes of the bank were all paid in full soon after the failure.

The following table gives average paid up capital, assets, liabilities, and other particulars of the various banks in operation in the years 1870, 1880, 1890, and 1893, since Confederation, according to the returns made to the Government as required by the Bank Act.

Year.	Capital Paid Up.	Notes in Circulation.	Total on Deposit.	Total of Discounts to the People.	Liabilities.	Assets.
1870	$33,031,249	$15,149,031	$48,763,205	$66,276,961	$65,685,870	$103,197.103
1880	60,052,117	22,529,623	85,303,814	102,166,115	111,838,941	184,276,190
1890	59.974,902	32,834,511	135.548,704	153,301,335	173,207,587	254,546,329
1893	62,009,346	33,811,925	174,776,722	205,623,042	217,195,975	302,696,715

www.ingramcontent.com/pod-product-compliance
Lightning Source LLC
Chambersburg PA
CBHW031443270326
41930CB00007B/841

* 9 7 8 3 3 3 7 1 1 7 3 3 7 *